IMPOSSIBLE TO BELIEVE

Memoir of an American Schoolboy

by Jack Coe

BREAKNECK HILL PRESS
Los Angeles, California

ISBN: 979-8-9907216-2-3

CONTENTS

PREFACE

The events in this book took place over fifty years ago. Writing about my experiences in prep school had been in the back of my mind for a long time, but it wasn't until I read something in 1991 that I knew I had to try to set the record straight someday. Or my record, at any rate.

Obey your teachers.
　　—My mother

It all depends on whose ox is getting gored.
　　—My father

The friends you make at Taft will become your best friends in life.
　　—My grandfather

I am left with the question of whether you ever mentioned any
　　of this to any adult in the community?
　　—Mr. John Esty, Taft headmaster 1963-1972

Don't be such a prude.
　　—Mr. Walter Marx, Taft master 1966-1970/71

On my tricycle, Breakneck Hill, Middlebury, Connecticut, 1958

The letter I was half dreading and half expecting came in late June 1971. Correspondence from the Taft School came in two sizes. A thick envelope meant acceptance. I'd received one of those in the spring of 1968. That one came with a warm, typewritten congratulatory welcome, along with several forms to fill out and mail back. The thinness of this one told me that Mr. Barnard's prophecy had come true. I left it on the dining room table for my parents to open. It was addressed to them, after all. I walked down to Sunset Boulevard and hitched a ride to the beach. The finality of it was starting to sink in. I needed a good wave-pounding baptism to get it all out of my mind for a while. It was early afternoon, a beautiful, warm sunny day in Santa Monica. "June gloom" had not yet arrived in the City of Angels. I knew a much deeper gloom would be waiting when I got back.

It was nearly dark when I got home. My trunks were still damp. My mother looked up at me from her chair when I walked in. Her eyes were red and her nose was dripping. The letter, opened and read, sat in front of her on the dining room table. Her failure as a mother, shedding white beach sand on her nice, blue carpet, standing in front of her. With nothing to say. Just a goofy smile on his face. My face. A face she didn't seem to recognize. After all we've done for you, her eyes told me. Giving you the opportunity for a first-class education. A head start in life. A chance to be someone special. Why would you throw that all away? To become a beach bum? A dropout? Those aren't in the family genes — on either side. She was right as rain about the last part. I was the thirteenth John Allen Coe on my father's side, and mother's side was full of high achievers. A lot was expected of me. From me.

But I looked like someone who begged to differ. And felt that way, too. My stomach was growling and I had goose bumps. It gets chilly in Los Angeles after the sun goes down. Worse if your trunks are still wet and you're starving. All I wanted was a shower followed by a hot meal and then bed. Why did life have to be more complicated than that? It didn't. And sometimes it was better not to complicate it too much. I could tell my mother a thing or two about that. And my father, too, when he got home from work. Which would be any minute. And so I excused myself and went and took a long hot shower. Yet another reminder of how dependent I was. Sponging off their hot water, their heat, their electricity, their house, their food – who wouldn't take me for a spoiled ingrate, knowing the resentment I felt toward my parents? Which I found to be savagely funny instead of the wake-up call it should have been.

I might have felt guilty about all that. Or should have. Except I didn't. I was just aware of it. Aware of a lot more than they knew. Or needed to know. Or would want to know. My failure was in the letter. I'd deal with that later. My success? That wasn't in the letter. I couldn't let them know about that. Not for a long, long time, if ever. It was a complicated story and I was years away from fully understanding it myself.

PART 1

This Was

CHAPTER 1

B efore I get to the heart of this story, there are some facts and background you should know.

I am the only son of an only son, born in Waterbury, Connecticut, June 1954. One of my sisters was 5 then, the other 7. My father was sales manager for the American Brass Company in Waterbury. His father was the president. American Brass was a division of a larger company called Anaconda Brass and Copper. From what I've heard, my great grandfather (dead before I was born) had started out as a machinist in upstate New York before becoming president of American Brass in the 1920s or 1930s.

By the standards of Middlebury, a rural suburb, we were a comfortably upper-middle-class family. To make room for me, we had just moved into a new four-bedroom gray-shingled Cape Cod house on top of Breakneck Hill. Though we were well short of rich, we didn't want for anything. To stretch the family budget, my mother avidly collected Blue Chip and S&H Green stamps. To get us to finish our dinner, especially the dreaded frozen chow mein that made the rounds every few weeks, she'd remind us to "remember all the starving children in China." My mother liked to garden way more than she liked to cook.

My mother and father engaged, 1944

My father met my mother while he was stationed at Moffett Field in San Jose during World War II. My mother was born in Eureka, California, and her parents were both from Garberville. Garberville was a rough-and-tumble pioneering town in the early 1900s, two hundred miles north of San Francisco, near what is called the Lost Coast. They were in grade school together and, as the story goes, my maternal grandfather had already made up his mind to marry my grandmother by then. His father died young and my grandfather quit school in the eighth grade to help support his younger siblings.

This grandfather eventually became manager of a bank in Eureka and gained the attention of A. P. Giannini — president of the Bank of America. Soon after, my grandfather moved his family from Eureka to Berkeley. My mother met my father when she was a senior at the University of California at Berkeley. While I was growing up on the East Coast, we rarely saw anyone on my mother's side of the family, so I knew little about them.

My memories of growing up in Middlebury are almost all good. I loved being outdoors and exploring the woods around our house. I didn't mind being indoors either. I had wooden blocks and train tracks. I could spend all afternoon in my room building elaborate cities with arching triple and quadruple train overpasses. My mother would come in every so often and put on a record to feed my imagination and architectural genius — everything from Gilbert and Sullivan to the theme song from *The Adventures of Rin Tin Tin*. I suspected it was just a matter of time until word leaked out, and I was put in charge of designing all the great future cities of the world.

I had lots of childhood friends, mostly boys my age like Jon Davie, Allan Sperry and Alec Bryan, but I was also very fond of Gigi Bowen, who lived just across the street from us on Breakneck Hill. I suppose she was what you would call a tomboy, blond and cute. We were the about same age, and by the time we were 4 or 5 years old we were fast friends. She was braver than I was and especially fearless around horses. We both loved the outdoors and exploring. I was a daydreamer, so it was easy for me to imagine a future with her. We did everything together. Her family had a horse barn and on lazy summer days we might go up to the hayloft to smooch. Or she'd throw a halter and bridle on

Grasshopper ("my" horse) and Daddy Longlegs (hers) and we'd go bareback riding in the meadows around Breakneck Hill. There was a one-room, dilapidated shotgun shack at the edge of one of those fields where we would sometimes dismount and tie up the horses. It was secluded, partly shaded by the limbs of an old crabapple tree, and as with any old, evil, scary looking place, we were naturally drawn to it.

Peering in we saw little except broken glass and a few old shell casings on the floor. You could tell the place had seen things we weren't ready to know about, and yet, after stopping by it a few times it began to seem less dangerous. And since no one else appeared to be using it, it came to feel like our secret hideaway. So much so, in my mind, that I eventually worked up the nerve and talked Gigi into taking off our clothes when we were there one afternoon. After breaking that taboo, I picked up a rock and broke one of the few remaining windows for the thrill of doing something else I knew I could get in serious trouble for. As we let the sun warm our bodies, I sneaked a look over at Gigi. She appeared to be nervous about getting caught, too. Meanwhile something in the back of my reptilian brain told me that while it might *seem* possible, I couldn't picture how my thing and her thing were supposed to work together. The sun was starting to get lower. The more shadows it cast around the shack, the less safe it felt. We put our clothes on and rode back to the barn.

A few weeks later, my father asked me about breaking the window at that shack. I wasn't worried about the window as much as I was terrified that someone had seen us naked. I thought I might get burned at the stake for that. It turned out run-of-the-mill vandalism was all I was accused of. I finally admitted it and received a severe scolding. For several weeks afterward I kept waiting for the other shoe to drop, but the afternoon Gigi and I spent in the Garden of Eden never came up.

By age 5 or 6 I had begun to notice that attractive adults tended to be nicer than those who were not. Both Gigi's mom and mine were good looking and they not only allowed but encouraged us to play together. Gigi's father, on the other hand, was fierce looking, a brutally handsome man's man. Sometimes when he looked at me, I got the feeling he wanted to take me out behind the woodshed for spending too much time alone with her.

Gigi had a brother, Rip, a couple years older than us. Rip had high-end toys like go-karts, cherry bombs and loud model planes with miniature motors that ran on some kind of rocket fuel. When Rip's better angels were out, he'd invite me over to show off what new gadget he had. When his dark angels were out, he would turn moody. And then after making sure there was no one around to prevent it, he'd bully me — like the time he made me walk his bicycle back up Breakneck Hill before my hernia operation at age 6 had fully healed.

Despite her father and brother, I assumed Gigi and I would get married, just as our parents had gotten married. That seemed to be the normal course of events when you got older. I was already thinking about constructing a real log cabin, like the toy log cabins I built in my room, only bigger and better. I wanted to cut right to the chase and get a head start in life. We would be free and self-sufficient and live off the land. I would dig a couple of deep pits on the animal trails nearby and cover them with twigs, moss and leaves. Game would fall right in. I'd light

A fuzzy picture of me kissing Gigi Bowen in the backyard of our home on Breakneck Hill in Middlebury, Connecticut, probably in 1959.

the charcoal grill outside while Gigi took care of the rest. There were a few gaps in my thinking of what the future would be like, such as where we were going to get the electricity and the television to watch *Bonanza* and *The Wonderful World of Disney* on Sunday nights. But what were parents for if not to make their children's dreams come true? Life didn't have to be complicated and it wasn't back then. Not for me anyway.

While waiting for the right time to tell my parents where on the property I wanted to build my log cabin, one of the best things actually happening was my father reading me stories from the side of my bed before bedtime. My favorites were Dr. Seuss (*Myrtle the Turtle* and *Cat in the Hat*), and *Uncle Remus.* I also liked the North Wind stories from the book *East of the Sun and West of the Moon: Old Tales from the North*, a collection of Norwegian stories in translation. I would beg my father not to stop and sometimes grab onto him so he couldn't leave. It wasn't just that the stories were great. They were. It was his undivided attention that was so reassuring and comforting. Hard to believe I would soon hate my father for putting me in a place that would turn out to be worse than if he had left me chained alone inside the shotgun shack. A place I'd already seen, and not more than five miles away from where he read to me and fed my dreams.

As good as things were, in my imagination there was no reason they shouldn't get better. I was a post-World War II white American child, enjoying prosperity, optimism and comfort on a level never seen before and that possibly may never be seen again. While the gap may have been closing, where we lived nature still had the upper hand over man. It made for a healthy balance and rhythm to life. A major snowstorm would strand everyone at home, and then Middlebury's public works would deploy valiant snowplows to try to get everyone back to school or work. On a cold winter day waiting to get into a car in our driveway, even the exhaust out the tailpipe smelled like great progress to me.

I was curious about everything. I once found two insulated electrical wires in the basement and stuck them in a socket. I thought long and hard about touching the two exposed copper "snake tongues" to find out what would happen. Another time I was sleeping over at my best friend Jon Davie's house. After waking up early, I opened one of his eyelids just to see what a sleeping eye looked like.

I was warily curious about God and the Devil after hearing about them in church. If there really were two competing powers floating around in control of everything, including me, I wanted proof. If something wasn't going my way, I'd go down to the basement and repeat the word "hell" (which was the most dangerous word I knew) fifty to a hundred times to summon a visit from either one. I eventually gave up, figuring either they didn't exist or I wasn't important to them.

We were Protestant, or Episcopalian, and my father dutifully drove us all to church in Watertown every Sunday. I liked the drive over because my father often let me sit in his lap and steer the car. I did not like getting out of the car. Church was too serious and somber. Knowing when to stand, sit or kneel, figuring out what page we were on in which book, when it was time to sing a hymn, or reply to the white-haired minister in his strange-looking robe and pointy hat like in a game of Simon Says, or when to say "amen" — it was all extremely confusing and made me feel like a dunce. I would wear my play clothes underneath and wriggle out of my Sunday suit in the back seat of our car, waiting for my parents to quit gabbing so I wouldn't miss an extra minute of playtime or adventure when we got home.

CHAPTER 2

D riving home from church, my father would sometimes take a route past a place that made my eyes open wide. Fronting the road was a long curving white split-rail fence. Beyond that were vast lawns and stately trees. Further back, red-orange brick buildings seemed to have sprouted out of the ground and risen like the city of Oz. Had this place been closer to where we lived, my friends and I would have spied on it — much like we did peering down from our redoubt on South Street as giant earthmovers gouged a wide scar through pristine wilderness to make way for Route 84. To see for ourselves what went on there and whether we liked it. If we didn't, we'd report back to our parents to sound the alarm.

It was obviously a place of great importance. After my parents told me what it was, they laughed when I said in all seriousness that I would never be big or old enough to attend a school like that.

After graduating from nursery school with a special award for "best napper," I did not particularly like moving up to the rigors of Shepardson Elementary School. I didn't like being cooped up in a classroom under fluorescent lights when there were so many more interesting things to do outdoors. I was sent to the cloakroom numerous times in first grade for acting up. I would count the holes in the square ceiling tiles before being called back in by Miss Malone. I got in a fair amount of trouble once after she briefly left the classroom. I stood and told the rest of the class that Miss Malone was "a crummy teacher with crummy looks." Rachel ratted me out. Rachel, a fellow first-grader and much better student than me, had a small scab above her lip that looked like the fatty crackle on the edge of a juicy steak. It was all I could do to keep from asking her if she could peel it off to satisfy my curiosity — willing to forgive her for ratting on me if she would.

We occasionally would go on field trips like one we took to a dairy. I liked field trips because they allowed a peek into the future after school dress rehearsals were over. You could tell a lot just by watching the workers. If they smiled back, they were letting you know the job wasn't all that bad. That helped me think about what lay ahead more than school did.

Our house was on a level stretch of road at the top of Breakneck Hill. Our street got its name during the Revolutionary War when an ox broke its neck while going down the hill when the cannon it was pulling careened out of control. There was a hodge-podge of narrow, overgrown footpaths that crisscrossed the woods and fields around that part of Middlebury. They were dotted with polished granite markers where American Revolutionary soldiers had once bivouacked for the night. I liked the idea that a ragtag group of boys and men from my home state had the bravery and wherewithal to outfox the more organized British redcoats. I thought we could have used a little more of that same fighting spirit to be free of the twin tyrannies of church and school, but I seemed to be a minority of one in that regard.

On warm summer nights my father would set up a telescope in our backyard and we would take turns looking at the moon. On other clear moonless nights, he would point out the constellations, and occasionally Sputnik — the Russian-made first satellite in orbit — winking like a firefly as it slowly traveled east to west across the night sky. During the Cuban Missile Crisis in 1962, our cleaning lady and her husband were babysitting me and said we

With my sisters in the backyard of our home on Breakneck Hill, Middlebury, Connecticut

were about to go to war with Russia. I wasn't worried. I knew America would win. We'd never lost a war yet.

The L.L.Bean catalog came out once a year and I would salivate over the outdoor gear, but what I liked most were the ruggedly handsome knives. By the time I turned 7, I had a small knife collection and would practice throwing my Jim Bowie knife at a tree in our backyard with little success.

My father stood about 6'2" and was a handsome man. He was the disciplinarian in the family. When my sisters or I misbehaved, my mother would let him do the honors with a hairbrush on our behinds when he got home from work. Owing to his father's and grandfather's positions at American Brass (my grandfather retired as vice president of Anaconda and chairman of American Brass in 1962 but still worked as a consultant for both companies), my father was on the fast track to a managerial position. As a salesman, he would often travel for a week at a time to cities like Chicago and Detroit. Anaconda manufactured copper sheet that went into car radiators and other products including wire and copper and brass tubing. He took pride in his job and appearance. There was a room in our basement filled with Kiwi shoe polishes and an electric buffer. He had boxes of hats to go with half a dozen suits. Our father did not talk politics with us, but in 1960 there was a large photograph of him on the front page of the *Waterbury Republican* proudly shaking hands with a beaming Richard Nixon as a Connecticut delegate at the Republican National Convention.

My father would occasionally wake me up very early on a Saturday to go fishing. We would stand in the middle of the Pootatuck

River, where I would struggle to maintain balance against the current and slippery rocks, trying to keep the freezing water from lapping over my waders, a smelly creel bag tied around my waist. I would have rather stayed in bed until the sun was up and the smell of bacon and waffles drifted into my room, but I understood he was trying to teach me things a boy should know.

Beginning in 1962, my father started traveling regularly — two weeks away followed by two weeks at home. My mother would show us where he was on a US map that hung on our kitchen

With my sisters in the backyard of our Los Angeles home before church, January 1964.

wall. He was going to the same place every time — all the way to the other side of the country. At the end of that year, he asked my sisters and me what we thought about moving to Los Angeles. None of us wanted to leave Middlebury, but it wasn't really a question. It was an announcement.

The Mayflower moving company arrived soon after. Strange men invaded our home and began putting blue stickers on every stick of furniture we owned. They spent days dollying all our things up a ramp and cramming them into a van that looked three school buses long. If this was all being done to rattle me, the plan was working. It unsettled me, all right. Middlebury was my home and in my bones. I was in no way done exploring its mysteries or ready to leave my friends behind.

My parents were going to drive the station wagon to Los Angeles while my sisters and I would stay at my grandparents' house and fly out after our parents settled in. A few days before their departure, I had a sleepover with a friend who came down with chicken pox or measles. In order to not expose my grandparents, the plan changed. My sisters would fly out and I would drive across country with my parents.

The journey began with me begging them to stop only at Howard Johnson restaurants and stay only at Howard Johnson hotels. My insecurities were on high alert. To distract me, my mother would drill me with addition, subtraction, multiplication and division flashcards while my father drove. For fun we would play a game of picking which type of car on the interstate was the most popular. I always took VW Beetles and won every time.

After we crossed either the Missouri River or the Mississippi, Howard Johnson establishments petered out, and we started staying at Best Western hotels. It took three days to drive across Texas. My mother's back went out during that stretch and I had to trade places with her so she could lie flat in the rear of the wagon.

We didn't do much sightseeing except for brief visits to Hoover Dam and the Grand Canyon. Looking out the car window, I was shocked at how arid, flat and empty the landscape was. I'd watched a lot of *Bonanza* on television, so that was my idea of what the West was like. So much for that illusion. Not a single cowboy, Indian or pine-studded hill in sight. Even the cactus looked miserable; stuck in the middle of nowhere under a broiling sun. As we drove across the Mojave Desert, my father followed the lead of several motorists and purchased a desert bag that he filled with water. He strapped it to the front of the car to keep the engine from overheating.

We limped into LA after dark and checked into the Bel Air Sands Hotel near the junction of the 405 freeway and Sunset Boulevard. I woke up the next morning and opened the curtain. It was February — snow fort building time in Middlebury or maybe ice skating at Turtle Pond with hot chocolate — and gaped at a young woman as she strolled around a pool while breastfeeding her baby beneath a canopy of palm trees, blue skies and a warm Santa Ana wind.

Had we stayed in Connecticut, there were rumblings that my parents were going to send me to an all-boys private day school. I was in the middle of third grade when we left, and while I was getting used to school being a fact, I still preferred exploring, being outdoors and daydreaming. Part of me wished the Revolutionary War was still going on so I could have something more exciting and important to do than learn the 3 Rs. When my sisters told me I had at least nine more years of school ahead, my inner Davy Crockett was bitterly disappointed.

Our new home was in Pacific Palisades. It was (and is) one of the nicer parts of Los Angeles, minutes from the beach, but the houses were practically on top of one another. With no woods to get lost in, I felt like a cat on a beach with no place to hide. Right away I had a big problem fitting in, with no natural defenses against the neighborhood boys who were eager to put this new kid with a strange accent and kooky crewcut to the test. My next-door neighbor and another boy teamed up to knock me down in front of my mother as I was helping her unload groceries in the driveway one afternoon. I would have loved to put on my coonskin hat, take out my Jim Bowie knife and hurl it end over end deep into the trunk of the nearest palm tree, splitting it in two. Unfortunately, I had not mastered that skill.

I went to Canyon Elementary School, where I faced similar treatment. I had never had to fight before but quickly realized that if I was going to be accepted, I would have to change who I was. I stopped backing down and began looking for fights at the slightest provocation. I started acting up in class when I discovered that it made me more popular, too. Once I earned a reputation as a class clown and a frequent visitor to the principal's office, most of my immediate problems went away. I was able to relax and stop looking for fights now that I had a new group of friends — a group that strangely included many who had tested me.

My parents bought me a guitar for Christmas in 1964. It was an inexpensive nylon-string Orpheus acoustic that came in a black cardboard pebble case. My mother signed me up to take weekly group lessons with a free-spirited woman who lived in Santa Monica Canyon. She taught us folk songs like "Hang Down Your Head Tom Dooley." I did not like going to lessons at first — it was just another commitment that cut into free time that I'd rather spend daydreaming or playing with marbles in my bathtub or gluing together a Big Daddy Roth model car or bothering our cat. But something about the guitar struck the proverbial chord in me. I found myself gravitating to it even when I didn't have to practice for the weekly lesson. The sound soothed me and slowly got a hold on me even though I got frustrated when I didn't play something perfectly or didn't hold the strings down tight enough, making it sound muted and ugly instead of clean and nice.

Becoming a Southern Californian didn't happen overnight. When I was 10, I etched "Go Yankees!" on the cover of my school note-book as a reminder of my East Coast roots. I don't think I realized just how much I was acclimating to Los Angeles until my father's parents came for a visit. Nannie and Bobby (as they were known to me and my sisters) were dyed-in-the-wool New Englanders, and their visit seemed less like a vacation than a reconnaissance mission to see if our pilgrimage to California was undermin-ing their early influence and Puritan values. Looking hot and bothered in their wool suits, they grimaced at the sight of their grandchildren running around in shorts and tank tops — using words like "bitchin" to describe the balmy winter weather, eating tangerines off the tree in our backyard and playing ping pong in the lanai between dips in our heated pool. My father remained tight-lipped throughout, bending over backward to make them happy while reminding the three of us to act more civilized and respectful in their presence. We were all relieved when they went back to Connecticut, no one more than my mother.

My friends and I tended to look up to and take our cues and lumps from older kids who were spearheading a youth movement. Southern California was a hotbed of American youth culture at that time, with souped-up cars, surfing, skateboarding (aka sidewalk surfing) and surf music. That wasn't where my roots were but I was quick to adjust. A sense of entitlement and invincibility went hand in hand with our pleasure-seeking. After President Kennedy was assassinated, I was miffed that my favorite TV shows were pre-empted by his funeral. Where adults seemed apprehensive about the future (several homes in my neighborhood had bomb shelters that we would raid for chocolate bars when the Helms Bakery or Good Humor trucks were late), we were all about having fun and seeking new ways to find more. Time was on our side and we lived for today. None of us saw dark clouds on the horizon.

I had no real appreciation for my father or understanding of what he did at Anaconda's copper tube plant in Paramount, which was a suburb on the other side of Los Angeles from where we lived. I was too wrapped up finding my own way and trying to fit in. And when he gave me advice about life, it was usually along the lines of "most men lead lives of quiet desperation," "the mills of the Gods grind slowly but exceedingly small," "marriage is hard work" and other New England chestnuts that seemed out of place and out of time on the west side of Los Angeles.

My bedroom on Corsica Drive was upstairs. I had the whole second floor to myself. Down the hallway the furnace and water heater had a room of their own, often scaring me at night with their strange noises. I knew the boogeyman lived there, and I spent many nights with the bedcover half over my head waiting in dread for his murderous appearance at my door after my mother or father kissed me goodnight.

There was a large playroom upstairs with a television and a couple of couch-beds which I could retire to after school with a bag of barbeque potato chips and a carton of orange juice to watch surf movies on Channel 5 followed by *Divorce Court*, *Leave it to Beaver* and then *The Many Loves of Dobie Gillis* until dinnertime. The playroom had a large window that looked over the Riviera Country Club, where I took tennis and golf lessons. From that window I saw columns of black smoke rising from a safe if unsettling distance during the Watts riots in August 1965.

As he had in Connecticut, my father set up a basketball hoop above our garage door. It became a magnet for the boys in the neighborhood. Everyone played outdoors and our neighborhood was swarming with kids. Being driven to a play date was unheard of. We all had bicycles and simply walked, biked or skateboarded to someone's house, or down to Rustic Canyon Park to play whatever sport was in season. We had a spotlight that lighted our driveway at night, and we would play late into Friday and Saturday evenings — usually while listening to Chick Hearn announce Laker games over a transistor radio. Jerry West was a star on a very good Lakers team but they rarely beat the Boston Celtics with Bill Russell, John Havlicek, "Satch" Sanders and Sam Jones — and never when it counted. I became a huge

Laker fan, and by extension a lifelong fan of the underdog in any sport; and an ardent hater of Boston coach Red Auerbach and his victory cigars.

My favorite player was Elgin Baylor. I spent hours trying to copy his patented "double clutch" shot. My father would come out to show us his two-handed set shot, which made me cringe with embarrassment.

I developed a crush on Amy Sherman at Canyon Elementary School. She was smart, self-assured and pretty. My chief rival for her attention was Barry Michaels, the smartest boy in our class. He was assigned to escort me to the principal's office whenever I got into trouble, which only made me more determined to win her over. By the end of sixth grade, I'd managed to maneuver my original seat assignment to a spot next to hers, all without our teacher, Mr. Santel, noticing — or perhaps caring. When my next-door neighbor David Schiff, my sometime nemesis and sometime friend, told me there was an extra day or two of school vacation that year, I was disappointed by school again — this time because it meant one or two less days of playing footsies with Amy under our desks.

My mother was a stay-at-home mom. She had back fusion surgery in 1965, but that did not stop her from playing tennis or slow her down. Compared to football, baseball and basketball, tennis was considered a white-shorts sissy sport, but I enjoyed playing with her and the rest of the family on the canyon courts at the Riviera Country Club after school and on late summer afternoons. Except for church, tennis was the one activity we all did together. Looking back, our family tennis games, though few and far between at times, were the glue that held our family together in those years. My mom graduated Phi Beta Kappa from Cal Berkeley in two-and-a-half years and read the *New Yorker* and *The Atlantic*. She became more liberal as a result and was starting to question the Vietnam War although she was not yet outspoken about it. My parents' social circle was mostly conservative (Ronald Reagan lived just a few blocks north of us on Capri Drive) while my father, who didn't have the time to read as she did, was quietly conservative. Whenever one of us children would question America's shortcomings, such as why we were in Vietnam, his terse reply was "Name a better place."

The escalation of the Vietnam War and the deepening divisions in America, along with the threat of nuclear war with Russia (whenever it aired on television in the mid-sixties, my friends and I would watch the movie *Failsafe*, which played to those fears) were about the only bumps in the otherwise smooth ride of our youthful existence. And because those thorny problems were caused by adults, we didn't feel they were ours to solve. All we had to do was follow the musical advice of the Beach Boys, Jan and Dean, the Surfaris, et cetera, and the rest of America (and the world) would surely come around and realize our way was better than theirs.

I have a vague memory of my mother throwing a pot at my father when I went into the kitchen early one morning in Connecticut when I was a child, but otherwise I rarely heard them fight or argue. They were the two-headed monster when it came to parenting, always on the same page. They were tough to deal with one-on-one. They married young (my father was 22 and my mother was 20) and as the sixties wore on and the world was shifting around them in ways they probably could not have imagined, they became more unified than ever. I sometimes found myself wishing they would get divorced, believing that would give me more freedom to do the things I wanted.

My mother found a calling in 1966. It was an ad hoc organization called Cookie Day, with several mothers from the neighborhood getting together to bake cookies to send off along with letters of support, paperbacks and comic books to lift the spirits of our troops in Vietnam. When it was my mother's turn to host, I would come home after school to help the ladies seal the cardboard boxes with their strange, foreign destinations like Da Nang and Saigon.

In the fall of 1967, I entered Paul Revere Junior High. My sixth-grade class of some thirty-five students merged into a class of about 600 from several elementary feeder schools. Seventh-graders were known as scrubs, bottom of the heap. Between classes and during nutrition and lunch breaks, scrubs had to look out for older boys who could scatter your textbooks to the ground and earn you a tardy slip if you were late to your next class. I had friends and was starting to make new ones. I was no longer looking for fights — especially against older, bigger boys I couldn't beat. That said, there were some situations I could not avoid. One older boy who was repeating math made me slap fight with him almost every day before class. That was probably karma for the slap fights I made our cat at home engage in. Another lunkhead walked up to me one morning with a group of his friends during nutrition break. He was going to show them how to fake hocking a loogie at someone and he hocked a real one in my face. Howls of laughter.

I was very slender and my sisters' friends often said they wished their eyelashes were as long as mine. Older, tougher boys naturally liked to pick on weaker boys. That prompted me to start doing pull-ups and push-ups every night. I didn't want to get sand kicked in my face by the beach stud on the back cover of the Superman and Archie comics.

California public schools were considered very good back then. Teachers maintained order. If you misbehaved, you had your choice of detention or (for boys) swats. I chose a couple of swats in lieu of detention once. The instruction that the boy's vice principal, Mr. Adler, gave me after he closed the door to his office was rather dry. He told me to bend over, hold still and stare at the little red dot on the wall just above the floor. He picked up a large wooden paddle and warned me not to put my hand back to protect my butt under any circumstances or it might get broken. Two swats later, he shook my hand and there were no hard feelings. It was one of those rites of passage in junior high that gave me something to tell my friends about.

In addition to English, math and science, there were classes in journalism, typing, metal shop, drafting and agriculture. There were after-class programs for sports, and dances with live bands in the gym Friday nights. Mirroring real politics, we had elections for student body offices. Earning a landslide victory, Larry Blivas began his speech with "I feel like a mosquito at a nudist colony — I don't know where to begin." He won in a landslide. My best friend Preston Iverson was elected lower division class president on his good looks and personality.

Below the surface there were things going on that teachers didn't know. The two toughest boys chose each other off. Word spread throughout the day and half the school gathered to watch them duke it out after class in a dry culvert (we called them barrancas), where they stalled by arguing whether martial arts were allowed until the boys' vice principal came to their rescue. It was good theater.

PART 2

Getting to This

CHAPTER 3

A new family arrived in our neighborhood around 1965. The father had been a college track star. Black and white photographs of him in a tank top, holding javelins and vaulting poles lined the walls of their home. They had three boys all around my age. Mr. Van Sant was very keen on passing his love of sports and competition to his boys and the rest of us. He built a pole vault pit in their backyard, the physics of which I could never comprehend. He made an enthusiastic pitch to several parents in the neighborhood to send their sons (along with his) to Bob Mathias Sierra Boys Camp in Kings Canyon National Park in Central California. I was not keen on camp but my parents prodded me into going.

There were about a hundred boys for each six-week session. We were divided by age and assigned a cabin with double bunk beds and a counselor. Bob Mathias was an Olympic decathlon gold medal winner in 1952 and 1956. He was a towering man and the pride of Tulare, a small farming town downhill from the national park in the High Sierra where his camp was held. He starred in two movies: *The Bob Mathias Story* (an inspirational weeper) and *The Minotaur*, which was one of the better "camp" movies ever made.

The camp was very structured with outdoor activities that began before the sun came up and there was still frost on the ground. The triangular bell would ring up at the main lodge and we would hurry down to circle the flagpole for the raising of the Stars and Stripes and to recite the Pledge of Allegiance, hands over our hearts. That would be followed by about twenty minutes of calisthenics. After breakfast, we'd divide into groups and make the rounds to the archery and rifle ranges, the trampoline pit, the high jump and so on. Outdoor church services were held in a clearing where the head counselor wisely taught that God was in nature and not in organized religions. After that we were free to read comics, make lanyards, buy corn nuts at the commissary and write letters home.

The counselors were all in their late teens or early twenties, and for the most part they were very good and dedicated. One redhead had a Fender Stratocaster electric guitar. He would let me play it in return for a back rub. While I didn't like that part of the bargain, getting to play the Strat won out over the ick factor of rubbing his back. A devil's bargain that I did not think much of at the time but the memory would come back to haunt me in a few years.

One of my favorite things at camp was playing something called Russian baseball. There were few rules. Foul balls were fair game, pitchers pitched to their own teams, and second base was way out in centerfield. Once you made it to first base, you could pretty much go wherever you wanted when the next batter hit — up into the hills if you felt like it. After that the only rule was that you had to reach second base and then eventually home to score a run without getting tagged along the way. There was no third base and scoring thirty runs was no guarantee of winning. It was a lot more fun than the American version.

There was a large man-made lake behind the baseball field. On really hot days after dinner when it was still light out, the counselors would announce "skinny dip" and we would all run back to our cabins, shed our clothes and run naked down to the lake, screaming all the way. I liked the feeling of swimming naked — it felt free and natural — though I could have done without so much company.

In my second year they added log rolling on the lake. I was one of the best at it, but when the end-of-session "Olympics" was held, I fell off before making it to the final round. By my third and final year I had yet to be selected to receive a regular pine cone for being a "good camper," much less a silver or gold one for being one of the best.

One afternoon I was swimming next to the dock where the rowboats were tied when some boys started chucking crabapples at me. I decided to fake them out and swam underneath the murky water as far as I could go before surfacing. When I came up, my head hit one of the steel drums that supported the dock. I was out of breath and had no idea which direction to go to surface. If I chose the wrong way and came up under another barrel, that might be the end of me. When I did emerge, I was mercifully in the clear except for another barrage of crabapples.

For one week each session, we would be issued backpacks with packages of Bernard's dehydrated food and then trucked up to Kings Canyon for a grueling six-to-ten-mile hike into one of the back country's many majestic snow-fed lakes. We would arrive strung out, exhausted, and then set up our sleeping bags around the center of camp; the farther away from the counselors the braver you were.

After dinner we would make a campfire and one of the counselors would tell a story. A favorite was about the young sea captain whose hand had been bitten off by a giant wharf rat, leaving him with a hook, no job and a bitter outlook. He became the prime suspect in several gruesome attacks in San Francisco. Witnesses recounted a man with a hook who matched his description. Evading the manhunt, he'd escaped to the Sierra where he was rumored to be living in the wild, breaking into cabins to steal food. The counselor would end the story with a brief aside that some recent cabin break-ins were not far from where we were. The following morning, sleeping bags were practically on top of one another and as close to the counselors and campfire as they could be.

I was entered in the steeplechase event for the end-of-session "Olympics" my last year. The son of the head counselor was also entered. We had been in a wrestling match earlier that summer and he'd pinned me on the cabin floor in front of several boys. I was very motivated to beat him. It took every ounce of will, but as I crossed the monkey bars over the muddy creek that fed the lake and headed down the dirt road toward the finish line, I was in front and knew I was going to win. A tall, handsome black man waiting at the finish line asked for an interview. He turned out to be Rafer Johnson — a friend of Bob Mathias and fellow gold medal decathlon winner. I was too spent to notice there was a cameraman behind him. When it was over, he told me I would be on the 11 p.m. news that night back in Los Angeles.

I called my parents to let them know. As happened once before in Middlebury, when I told them a huge tree had come down in the woods behind our house, they didn't believe me — until a neighbor mentioned she had seen me on TV the next day. When they told me this after I got back from camp, they thought it was an amusing little story for the family lore. But I was bothered by it. That was twice they hadn't believed me about something I thought was important. It wouldn't be the last time.

Winning the race taught me some things. I had more inner strength than I thought but I also didn't care that much about winning and the praise that came with it. My bunkmates had outed me for whacking off a few weeks before even though I had taken great pains to conceal what I was doing by pretending I was drumming on my stomach under my sleeping bag. The same cabin mates who tried to yank off my sleeping bag and mocked my "drumming" story put me on a pedestal after I won the race. Overcoming that embarrassment was another motivation to win, but deep down I found it confusing: beating others was good but beating oneself for pleasure was not.

By the time I aged out of summer camp I'd grown very interested in girls. Pacific Palisades was founded by pious Methodist ministers in the early 1900s, but by the mid-sixties any threads from that era had been snipped by miniskirts and bikinis and cutoff jeans. At Friday night teen dances, teachers and parent chaperones would pace the sidelines as we writhed to live bands under a lightshow. They would occasionally wade in and break apart a couple bumping and grinding too close, but otherwise they left us alone. These dances led to weekend parties where we played games like spin the bottle and truth or dare. Looking back, the adults held the reins loosely. They seemed to understand the attraction between boys and girls was only natural.

By 1967, I felt at home in Los Angeles. I had a good group of friends. We played sports after school, went to parties and dances and spent the better part of the summer at the beach — alternating between bodysurfing in the cold Pacific and crawling on our stomachs like lizards in search of hot sand. Girls we knew from school would lay nearby in their bikinis, feverishly working on their tans while ignoring us. The parents of some of our classmates were in the movie business. Those kids had more room to roam. Their parties were often unsupervised. Stories would spread about the wild things they did. For those of us from more conventional homes, there were warning signs that our happy-go-lucky freedom was about to get a reality check in the opposite direction. Cotillion at the Bel-Air Bay Club was one such threat.

Parents, and in particular stay-at-home mothers like mine, started piling on the after-school activities like scouting to keep us busy. David Newman's mother made him practice violin an hour a day, whether he had friends over or not. Danny Bernstein, Jack Friedman and I had to attend a speed-reading class for four weeks in the summer of 1967. There were religious schools many of us had to attend once a week: "Jew School" for my Jewish friends like the Stoller twins, Jon and Roger, and confirmation class for

Episcopalians. Or Protestants. I was still confused about which branch we belonged to – and didn't care.

The more my parents focused on my future the more resistant I became. They wanted me to go to a quasi-military school in the San Fernando Valley that was then called Harvard. They took me for an interview that did not go well. After that they made an appointment with someone I suspect was a shrink. That did not go well either. I seem to remember he gave me a Rorschach test, and probably told my parents I had an inferiority complex. It would have been swell to think I was something special, but my track record in school proved that I was nothing more than an above-average student. You learn your place in a large public school pretty fast, and the best way to survive it is to blend in and find friends who reflect who you are. If I were suddenly to "apply myself" and become a bookworm and straight A student,

With my sisters at home in Los Angeles, circa 1967

I would lose all my friends. I did not like losing friends. All I wanted was to stay in public school, remain one of the gang, and be left alone.

Junior high school had its ups and downs but the ups generally outweighed the downs. Paul Revere had a 70/30 mix between standard academic and vocational courses, which meant that almost every student had something they could feel good about. I was a solid B student, always trying for A's and B+'s to please my parents but content to be what I was. I studied reasonably hard and I wasn't into cheating just to get a better grade on my report card. One of the last fights I had was with a friend I wouldn't let cheat off me.

I always got books for Christmas and birthdays, and despite my addiction to television, I liked to read. *Lizzie Borden: The Untold Story* was one of my favorites. I first read it when I was in fifth grade. What can I say in my defense except I found it on our bookshelf one day and it was a page turner. My father started locking the garden tool shed after that, but otherwise both my parents encouraged me to read. I read all the Hardy Boy books and other novels like *Old Yeller* and *Lad: A Dog*. At times I wished I had a dog to look up to me but the main breed in our neighborhood were poodles and many of them had little red bows tied around their necks. *Death Be Not Proud*, *Thirty Seconds Over Tokyo*, Eddie Rickenbacker, Jerry Kramer — my parents were always giving me books meant to inspire me and they did. I wanted to do something good with my life although I had no idea what.

CHAPTER 4

At the beginning of every school year my parents would tell me how important it was, that my grades would decide what classes I could get into the following year. Furthermore, good grades and advanced classes would determine what college or university I would or wouldn't get into. I didn't like the implication that without college I couldn't amount to much. My early childhood heroes like Daniel Boone, Davy Crockett and Jim Bowie didn't owe their success to higher education. And the boys who were looked up to in school were not the smartest. There was also the hanging threat that boys who didn't get into college were more likely to be sent to Vietnam. Although that was a long way off for someone my age, it seemed unfair and at odds with the morals in the books I read.

The older I got the more unclear I was about the future. The optimism of the California surf culture was beginning to show signs of distress. Several local surf legends were turning into hardcore surf louts — drinking and getting busted at pot parties that made the local newspaper. Parents like mine were afraid of the influence the counterculture was having on us. The message I got was to study hard, get good grades and attend college like everyone else — or pay a heavy price if I didn't. My choices in life seemed to boil down to inviting disaster by not doing well in school, and sailing the scholastic seas to wherever they led.

Playing guitar, listening to music, watching the Three Stooges, hanging out with friends, flirting with girls, going to dances and movies, playing basketball, bodysurfing and snow skiing — those were the things I liked doing by the time I turned twelve. The only "responsibly adult" thing I liked was physical work, like mowing the grass with our push mower, which allowed my mind to daydream while burning off my intake of Laura Scudder's potato chips and Ding Dongs. Physical work left me pleasantly tired and feeling like I'd done something useful. My parents didn't believe in weekly allowances, so I'd wash both their cars on Sunday afternoons for pocket change. You had to be 16 to get a work permit to caddy at the Riviera Country Club — where rumor had it you could get tipped $5 or $10 for eighteen holes. My friend and I broke into the administration office at Paul Revere, stole some work permits, forged signatures and went down to the caddy shack early Saturday and Sunday mornings — sitting next to grown men in a haze of cigarette and cigar smoke, waiting in vain to get called.

As our young entrepreneurial spirits awoke, we tried our hands at window washing but after several complaints about our work, we moved onto painting house numbers on curbs. My next-door neighbor's older brother, Michael Schiff, came up with the idea. We went door to door, dressed in sports jackets and ties, reciting our pitch that began with "Hello. I'm in an organization for summer jobs for youths." The vague warning of what we might otherwise be up to if we *didn't* have summer jobs was usually enough to get them to sign up. David's older brother eventually turned the enterprise over to us, but dreams of building a business empire painting house numbers on curbs came to a quiet end one afternoon when a cop pulled up and issued me a ticket for soliciting without a business license.

My father never took me to work and it never occurred to me to ask him. The town of Paramount was thirty-five miles from leafy Pacific Palisades. Paramount was a flat, industrial part of Los Angeles with lots of factories, machine shops and neighborhoods with small houses separated by chain-link fences. Not that I ever went there. It may as well have been a million miles away.

In our family it went unsaid that my father did what he had to do to pay the bills. In that way he was no different than most of the fathers in our neighborhood. He drove to work each morning and came home in the late afternoon, Monday through Friday. He never said much about his job at Anaconda and that troubled me. I wanted to have fun and like what I did when I got older. His one question to me at dinner, "So who did you have lunch with today?", became so automatic that it turned into a family joke that even he came to appreciate. My father had a great sense of humor, but between the winds of social change and his boss at Anaconda who forced our relocation to California, he must have had a lot on his mind. The old adages he liked to repeat to his children came from experiences he seemed to be trying to shield us from.

His parental duty often seemed to boil down to preparing us for adulthood. Showing us, by example, that hard work led to success, telling us that taxes, mortgage payments and utility bills were just around the corner — and reminding us that how well we did or didn't do in school would largely shape our outcomes in life. He also did "dad stuff" like taking me to some Rams football games at Los Angeles Memorial Coliseum. However, I didn't particularly like rowdy crowds, and felt somewhat guilty driving around poor neighborhoods to barter for a parking space on car-crammed lawns before the game.

My dad would get a few weeks off each summer and we'd go on family car trips. We went to a dude ranch in Montana one year and Glacier National Park another. I have few memories of those vacations because they seemed like calls of duty that didn't really bring us closer together as a family. At that point in my life, to feel more secure about the present I needed a connection to my past. The only time I got a glimmer of that was our summer of '64 trip to Garberville, where we camped with my mother's side of the family in the redwoods. I was surrounded by several aunts and uncles and fourteen or fifteen older first cousins I barely knew. After six weeks there (my father would commute the 600 miles back to work every couple of weeks) I felt like I belonged to a tribe for the first time in my life. Then in the winter of '64, the South Fork of the Eel River overflowed its banks and took out the orchard along with several acres of the bluff above the Eel where we used to camp, cook and play badminton and baseball. Our reunions ground to a trickle after that.

On April 4, 1968, my father came home from work, walked into the kitchen and told me and my mother that Martin Luther King

Jr. had been shot. There was little emotion in his weary voice but he had a concerned look. The Watts riots, a recent memory, were clearly on his mind. By then I had read the book *Black Like Me* — very popular at the nearly all-white Paul Revere. I was at a sports award banquet and watched as Kenny Batch, the only black boy in our school, and his father sat alone because no one would sit next to them. There is nothing so shameful as seeing something shameful and not having the courage to do something about it.

A few months later on June 6, my mother woke me up for school one sunny morning. She looked devastated, as if she'd been crying all night, and I braced myself for momentous life-changing news, like possibly that my father was dead. It turned out that Robert Kennedy had been shot in downtown LA and my mother had watched it unfold on television. They announced RFK's condition over the PA speakers at school for the next two days until he finally died from his wounds.

"And that's the way it is," as Walter Cronkite would say when he signed off on his popular evening newscast each night. John Kennedy, Martin Luther King and Robert Kennedy — all gunned down in the span of five years. America seemed to be coming apart, and no one had an explanation. Even the always reassuring "Uncle" Walter seemed to be at a loss. I was beginning to wonder where I would fit into such a society. I thought my only way out would come when I turned 18 and could start living life on my own. When I felt down, that dream would cheer me up. Until then, I would do the best I could, and try to avoid my parents whenever they brought up "my future."

By the time I turned 14 in 1968, the counterculture movement was in full bloom, or full anarchy, depending on your point of view. Resistance to the Vietnam war and the differences it exposed about race and the gap between the upper and lower classes fueled tremendous social unrest. If you could get into college, you could get a draft deferment. If you had money, you could pay a doctor to declare you unfit for military service. None of that seemed fair, but that was how the system worked. And there was no comfort in knowing it benefitted people of my socioeconomic class and skin color.

Growing up in Connecticut, I thought for sure that I would fight in a war someday. Back then, my mother read a lot of Greek and Roman stories to me, mostly passion plays about war, gods and heroes. Accountants and bank clerks were rarely mentioned. There were so many cultural references to war — in music, television, movies and toys in the 1950s and early sixties — that World War III seemed more a matter of when, not if. War wasn't necessarily on my mind when chowing down a peanut butter, jelly and marshmallow fluff sandwich on Wonder Bread followed by a box of animal crackers on a sticky August afternoon in Middlebury. But right after lunch we'd thread a fresh roll of caps into our toy guns and off my friends and I would go, back to our positions or forts, to hunt each other down. Until someone's mother came to pick them up, or the sugar wore off.

By 1968, Vietnam was not the "good" war I had envisioned fighting in when I was 6. A lot of older Americans, however, thought it was necessary in order to halt the spread of communism. The "red menace" and the "domino theory" were the buzzwords that hawks used to support the war. But as images of American casualties were starting to appear on nightly television along with occasional reports of American atrocities, the opposition grew.

I couldn't have been more confused. America had been "looked up to" since the end of World War II. The patriotic side of me wanted to believe we were in Vietnam for the right reasons. But it was starting to look like we weren't. The nightly newscasts as I remember them weren't really taking a position for or against the war so much as reporting on key battles or statistics like "body counts" on both sides — leaving viewers to make up their own minds about who was "winning."

Rock and roll was beginning to fill the void, at least for me. With the Beatles and Rolling Stones spearheading the British Invasion and American groups like the Jefferson Airplane, Buffalo Springfield, the Doors (and a hundred other bands and troubadours) filling the radio airwaves, I fell under the spell of their music. You had to read between the lines sometimes, but the messages had the ring of truth. Starting when I was 12 or 13, my middle sister was getting into nightly fights with my parents that were so loud that I had to turn up my radio to drown them out, furthering my appreciation of rock and roll. My little green molded plastic toy soldiers, with their machine guns and flame throwers sealed away in plastic bags buried in my closet, must have thought me a traitor as I strummed Beatle songs on my bed.

In early 1968 I learned we were moving back to Connecticut. Anaconda was transferring my father again. Greenwich would be our new home, about a two-hour drive from Middlebury. My father would take the commuter train into New York City. My sisters were in college and would stay behind in Los Angeles, sharing an apartment in Brentwood. I made my pitch to stay behind with them, promising to study hard, get good grades, sleep on their couch and not be a nuisance. I found a new calling in life: sincere desperation. I was about to enter ninth grade at Paul Revere in September. My friends and I would finally be at the top of the pecking order when it came to dances, sports and parties. I couldn't imagine anything worse than moving again, but that was only half of what my parents had in mind for me.

My parents brought up prep school. I had never read Charles Dickens, but I knew he wrote about bleak, bygone times, and nothing sounded bleaker or more bygone than boarding school. Where they served gruel for dinner and corporal punishment for dessert. Or maybe not. Maybe they were fancy, with white table cloths, silver service and butlers to cater to your every whim. When I found out they were all-boys' schools, I put my foot down. I was not going to sit next to a bunch of Nimrods and Poindexters while they ran Pythagorean circles around me. I wanted to continue sitting across from the likes of Nancy Slutsky, whose long legs and short miniskirts breathed some life into Miss Bradley's junior high geometry class.

If we had to move, the least my parents could do was let me go to a school rooted in the twentieth century. Greenwich was one of the wealthiest towns in America, so how bad could its public high school be? Bad enough, according to my parents who were getting the lowdown during their forays back and forth as they prepared for the move. Drugs were apparently "rampant" at Greenwich Country Day. I was not into drugs, but I was beginning to understand why many in my generation were.

I begged and pleaded to no avail. When my father made up his mind about something, he would become peevish. It was his way of declaring the discussion was over. After Easter break, my parents and I flew back East for a series of interviews at various prep schools, using my grandparents' house as home base for what I viewed as missions into enemy territory. Probably Hotchkiss, then Choate (I don't remember exactly what schools we visited) and finally nearest and dearest to my grandparents' hearts and home, the Taft School — the same school we'd pass by on Sundays after church in Watertown that I never thought I'd be big or old enough to attend.

Interviews, standardized-test scores and transcripts of my academic record at Paul Revere were required for acceptance. I don't recall whether I got accepted to any of the other schools, and I can only speculate why Taft let me in. At the end of each interview, an admissions officer would excuse my parents and then ask me why I so badly wanted to enroll. My answer did not seem to get through to them anymore than it did my parents.

I'm sure my grandparents had a lot to do with me getting into Taft and the decision to send me there. They were pillars of the community, with deep roots in Connecticut and Waterbury. When the Naugatuck River flooded in August 1955, my grandfather served on the Connecticut Flood Recovery committee — helping to rebuild the brass mills that had been one of the main sources of income and jobs in Waterbury. The flood was devastating. While my father and older sister watched from horseback as houses bobbed downstream from our backyard in Middlebury, water was pouring out second-story factory windows, leaving machinery covered with mud and ruined. Despite the rebuilding efforts, and also due to growing labor-management disputes, most of the brass mills in Waterbury and Naugatuck never fully recovered. When my grandfather died in 1987, the *Waterbury Republican* called him "one of the last of Waterbury's industrial giants."

My grandfather knew some of the administrators at Taft, probably from church or other social events. It's impossible to remain anonymous in a small town like Middlebury. I believe one he knew was Mr. Douglas, chairman of the math department, and the other, Mr. Cunningham, director of admissions. The only time Mr. Douglas spoke to me was during my upper mid-year. "Los Angeles just had an earthquake." This would become known as the Sylmar quake and it killed around sixty-five people. He knew I had family there, and that was all he had to say to me. For all I knew it was the "Big One" that Angelenos had been warned about for years. He looked at his watch, suggesting we were both in danger of being late for our next classes.

Likewise, veiny red-nosed Mr. Cunningham, always forward leaning with his hands clasped behind his back like Jiminy Cricket deep in thought, would nod a *keep up the good work* whenever he passed me in the main hallway with hardly a glance. In my grandparents' eyes (and to be fair, in the eyes of most upper-crust New England families then and probably now) prep schools were considered *de rigueur* for maintaining one's station in life. Public schools were for other stations, the kind that pumped gas and fixed flat tires. "The friends you make in prep school will become your best friends for life," my grandfather told me before I headed off to Taft, omitting that he had attended Crosby High — Waterbury's public high school.

My parents and I moved into a small, two-story rental house on Close Road in June 1968. Greenwich had woods, streams and green rolling hills like Middlebury but they all tended to be on closely guarded private property with mansions set deep behind imposing stone walls. It was hot, humid and demoralizing. The smells in the air were of cut grass, iced tea and freshly tarred two-lane roads. I tried skateboarding, but ended up getting honked at so many times that I quickly gave it up. On weekends I would beg my father to toss the football so I could work on my receiving skills. My father was more inclined to look at his ledger and balance his checkbook, but he spent many hours that summer throwing the football to me for overhead catches or just-off-the-grass fingertip grabs. I didn't want to show up at Taft like a fawn, the way I had when we moved to Los Angeles five years earlier.

My mother, meanwhile, was doing her part on the social engineering front. After several cross- country moves, she was adept at making new friends. My parents were introduced to other couples, either through their old Middlebury friends or my father's business associates. I was depressed and moped around the house. I didn't feel like making new friends. I lost them each time we moved. Making new friends in Greenwich seemed even more pointless because I was going off to Taft in the fall. But the more I lounged around our mustard-yellow house that summer, the more determined my mother became to get me engaged socially.

I proved extremely stubborn, but there were two set-ups I could not wriggle out of. One was a dress-up afternoon dinner party where the boys and girls decamped into separate rooms (the boys played billiards in the basement) before a bell dinged and all of us gathered around a formal dining room table where fondue was served in sterling silver pots with little Bunsen burners underneath. Having no clue what fondue was, I watched my better-bred peers dip chunks of raw filet mignon into pots with long silver forks and set them on their blue Wedgewood plates as they chatted away. Being hungry and left out of the conversations, I skipped the step of letting the meat cool and shoved a hunk straight into my mouth. As the flesh inside my cheeks sizzled, I managed to keep a straight face and act like nothing was wrong while taking in humiliating stares and whispers from around the table.

My mother's other failed attempt to put me on Greenwich's social map was to set me up on a blind date for a dinner dance at the country club. Arriving at a white marble Romanesque villa with a corsage in hand, I got out of the station wagon at my mother's insistence, after pleading with her to just honk the horn. I was pulling back on the big brass knocker when on the other side of the door I could hear my date screaming at her mother that she had no intention of going out with a loser like me and would ditch me as soon as her boyfriend arrived. I walked back to the car to tell my mother the good news when the front door slammed. My date stomped past me, a coiffed blond poodle whose seething looks I found strangely attractive. It was a tense, silent ride to the club. Good to her word, she disappeared the minute we arrived. I spent most of the evening sitting by myself at a large round table covered with white linen and doilies, listening to a twenty-piece orchestra swing through "Chattanooga Choo-Choo" and a host of other songs from a long, long time ago that my mother (and father) would know.

Taft piled on, too. The school assigned or suggested several books to read, *Mr. Chips* among them. My father had gone to Deerfield Academy in the 1930s but he didn't have much to say about his prep school experience other than that he respected and admired Frank Boyden, Deerfield's headmaster at that time. He told me about a boy in his class who had not been admitted but was dropped off at the school on opening day by his father anyway. Mr. Boyden took pity on the boy and let him stay. I hoped the opposite would happen to me, but getting out of Taft was looking more and more like a longshot. Although I continued to make my opposition known, the reply was that once I got over my prejudice, I would quickly learn to like Taft, just as I had summer camp, guitar lessons, and every other activity I'd initially resisted.

I received a letter from my "old boy," a senior at Taft who was supposed to take me under his wing. His name was Robbie Ford. I had to write him back. I wrote a letter and my mother reviewed it. I had not addressed him as "Dear Robbie" and had to write it all over again. I told her there was no way I was going to address some guy in an all-boys school with the word "Dear." It became one more argument I lost that summer and I ended up addressing Robbie as "Dear," wondering if ending the letter with "Very Truly Yours" was sincere enough. Perchance I should include a spray of freshly cut pansies in the envelope.

My sisters came out for a short visit that summer. We drove up to Middlebury to see some of our old friends, and hang out at the Highfield Country Club, which we used to belong to. My grandparents turned out to be very sensitive about who we were seeing and what we were doing in Middlebury, and this made it back to my parents, who passed the law down to us: There were to be no sleepovers with old friends. That would somehow reflect poorly on my grandparents. We would have to stay at their house, which resembled a museum, where I was constantly reminded that everything was breakable and irreplaceable. My best memory of that summer was driving with one of my sisters to Middlebury with the top down and the Doors "Hello, I Love You" breaking the sound barrier on the radio.

I found out that none of my old, close friends from Middlebury were going to Taft. Of the two Middlebury boys who were, Tad Redway and Chip Arnold, I had only vague memories. And they were attending as day students, not boarders. I met Bruce Maclean on a warm rainy night at perhaps the only party I went to in Middlebury late that summer. I didn't know him from before and didn't think much of him at first. He wore glasses and seemed a bit of a wise-ass. But the "bad" girls at the party — the ones standing out in the street with runs in their nylons, tight skirts and cheap mascara — were the kind that interested me. They hovered around Bruce as he doled out cigarettes. I bummed one myself and after a short conversation found out he was also going to Taft. He told me he was not looking forward to it, which made me feel a little better. I said I'd see him in a few weeks.

Eventually the day I'd dreaded arrived. I begged my parents to put me on a bus to preserve what dignity I had left. If I had to go, I wanted to arrive at the school gates under protest with my head held high. My father's reply, to paraphrase Eddie Cochran's "Summertime Blues," "No dice."

PART 3

Bugger's Banquet

I remember it being one of those classic New England late summer days when we arrived. Sunny but not too humid. Quite beautiful actually. My parents had won the battle of wills but lost me in the process. My father told me to smile and "cheer up" as I got out of the car. Good luck with that. A hateful smile was the best he was going to get. I was very good at holding grudges and this was shaping up to be a long one.

The grounds were undeniably grand. Inside the white split-rail fence that surrounded the front of the school were swards of the

View of the Taft School from the Taft/Watertown golf course

61

greenest, sweetest looking grass, with giant elm trees in broad leaf scattering dappled bits of shade and sunshine over the lawns. *Ferdinand the Bull* was not my favorite story growing up, but at that moment I wanted to follow his example: lay down on Taft's green clover and chew my cud until June rolled around. But on we walked to face judgment day.

Up close, the school buildings were even more magnificent than I'd remembered as a young boy or during my interview that spring. The facades were warm red-orange brick and mortar, several stories tall and adorned with climbing green ivy, all topped by steep, grey slate roofs that touched the sky at different points; giving the overall impression that, architecturally speaking, Taft was indeed a natural steppingstone to the Ivy League. Approaching the dining hall anteroom where we were to sign in and complete the formal enrollment process, a momentary sense of entitlement seduced me, and made me wonder if perhaps Taft might not be so bad after all.

While we waited in line to check in, I came back to my senses. Everyone around was gushing with excitement. I could understand my parents feeling that way on the cusp of getting me out of their hair, but what sort of boy can't wait for summer vacation to end and school to start? The anteroom was large, with stained glass windows on the east side, massive wooden beams overhead and a grand painting of the school's founder on the north wall. His eyes followed me wherever I went, signaling lofty expectations of a stern nature about to begin.

My worries grew as we waited for my incarceration to become official. Summer was coming to an end. It had not been a good one for me, but anything was better than the start of another school year — especially one with no girls around to blunt the misery. We were told my room was on the fifth floor of the HDT wing and instructed to take a creaky old freight elevator up to the fourth floor and then the stairs to the fifth. The man checking me in winked and said something to the effect that it must be my lucky day because "the Tower" with only three rooms on the entire floor was somewhat exclusive and offered one of the best views.

The stairs from the fourth-floor landing to the Tower were wooden and narrow. My father and I each took a handle of the trunk that held my belongings and we labored our way up with my mother following. The fifth-floor corridor was narrow and no more than twenty feet long. It was illuminated by two dust-moted shafts of sunlight that filtered through the two rooms on the right that faced southwest. The corridor was so dingy and cramped that any illusions I had of some posh, exclusive digs quickly shrunk. I would be spending the next nine months cooped up in what looked like a glorified attic.

A brief exploration revealed a communal bathroom at the end of the hall, just large enough for one person. The corridor continued to the right another ten feet before ending abruptly at a locked black steel door. With all means of escape cut off, I had no choice but to retrace my steps and face my parents' joy of settling me into the abyss.

My room was the first on the right, a double that I would share with Chip Wochomurka. I was hoping for a roommate with some street smarts who was as skeptical about all this as I was. What

I got was a pudgy, apple-cheeked boy from Weston, Connecticut, blushing with happiness and apparently looking forward to the nine-month lockup. As we shook hands under the gaze of our parents, he flicked his head to get a shock of strawberry blond hair off his forehead. My immediate impression was if push came to shove, I could take him. The second was that he could use a little dab of Brylcreem and the third was that all signs were pointing to us not getting along. The only question as our parents exchanged platitudes was who was going to be the top dog.

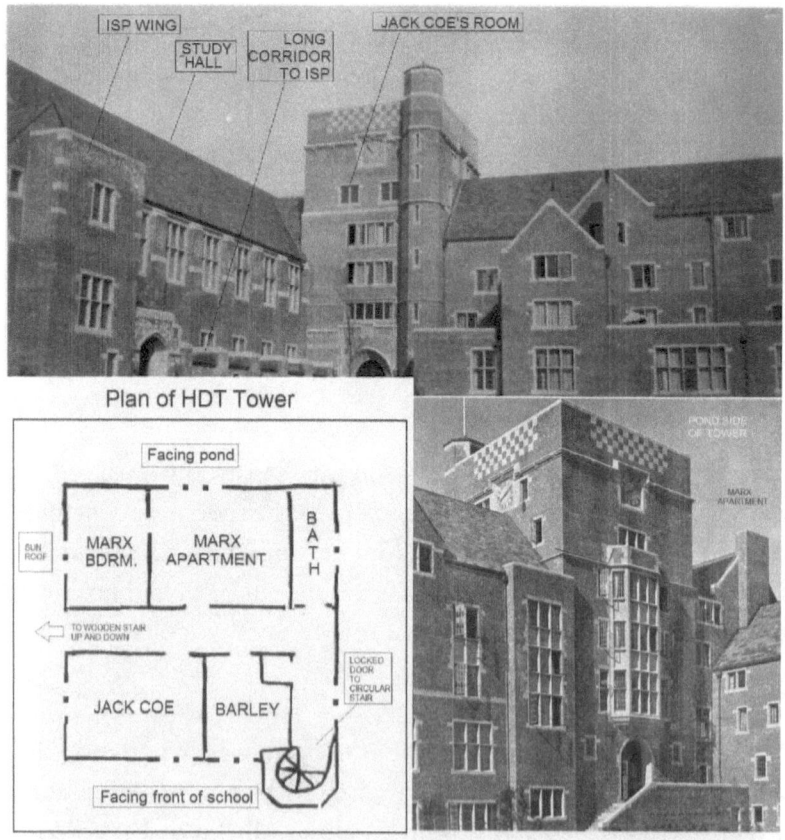

Plan of HDT Tower

The room next to ours was a single occupied by Willie Barley. Willie was a tall, black kid from Richmond, Virginia. He was smartly dressed, wore glasses and seemed serious and laconic at the same time. He struck me as a cross between a budding businessman and a young Malcolm X. We said our hellos in the hall and then he and his parents retreated into his room, perhaps to go over the do's and don'ts of navigating the upper echelons of the white world one more time. I can't remember if I met his parents as I was far more focused on losing mine.

Entering ninth graders at Taft were not called "ninth graders" or "freshmen." For whatever reason, we were called "lower mids." Sophomore tenth graders were "mids", eleventh graders were "upper mids" and seniors were sensibly called seniors. Teachers were called "masters" and the school principal was the headmaster. While the lower mid, mid and upper mid classifications sounded a little archaic, it was calling teachers "masters" that seemed strangest to me. As I had always heard it, the word "master" was usually followed by the word "servant." Semantics were the least of my worries, but I would learn that some teachers at Taft took "master" in the most literal sense of the word.

As my parents and Chip's continued to babble, I became even more sullen, which in turn forced my parents to work that much harder and longer to maintain the charade that I wanted to be there. It was then that the master of the fifth floor came tromping up the stairs. Mr. Marx announced his arrival by talking to his dog in a loud voice while ignoring us as he opened the door to his apartment across the hall. He let his decrepit Basset Hound skittle inside first and then closed the door behind them. He did not acknowledge any of us, which seemed odd to me. It was as though we had invaded his private realm. Several minutes passed before he came back out — either to introduce himself or see if he had frightened us off.

He was younger and taller than my father. He had a squiggle of thinning hair and wore heavy black plastic-framed glasses. His build was lanky but there was nothing fit or athletic about him. There was, however, a rather intense look in his eye; and the way his mouth turned up at the corners was halfway between a grin and a dare. *Underestimate me at your own peril*, his expression seemed to say. He wore a loud plaid sport coat that my mother would have vetoed in a heartbeat. The same went for the rest of his clothes, which looked like they came from a second-hand clearance rack. Part of me felt sorry for the way he looked. The

Walter Marx in 1966 or 1967

rest of me was dying to get into my old blue jeans, tee shirt and sneakers to try to restore my own shaken identity.

Parental attention turned to Mr. Marx to grease the final good-byes. He was not much help. He lacked what I called my parents' "company voice." His was too loud. And the more uncomfortable he became, the more he fidgeted, the louder it got. His social awkwardness seemed born out of a premature rush to get the chit-chat over with so he could get on with whatever it was he did. I will say that despite my first impressions, for someone about to take over parental duties, he did offer me one small ray of hope: I couldn't wait to get rid of my parents and Mr. Marx seemed to be of the same mind.

After my parents finally left, my "old boy" Robbie Ford paid me a visit later that afternoon. He was from Grosse Pointe, Michigan, and if he was related to the Ford Motor family in some way, or was aware that my father once sold copper sheet for his grand-father's radiators, we were several social tiers away from making that or any other connection. I already had on my trusty old jeans and tattered blue sneaks, while he was casually attired in a Brooks Brother shirt with a paisley ascot. Freshly ironed khakis with sockless topsiders rounded out his ensemble. He looked as though he'd just returned from an afternoon of yachting and had dinner reservations with the Titsenbaums. He seemed pressed for time, which was understandable given that I must have looked like a complete waste of prep school. He wished me luck and offered help if I needed any. I could tell by the way he said it, I'd have better luck looking under my bed for a lamp with a genie inside to get what I was wishing for. And so, my one and only meeting with my "old boy" was just that.

Chip and I finished putting our clothes away. I slid my guitar case under my bed, a cot made of squeaky sausage-linked springs underneath a thin mattress. I taped a poster of Bruce Brown's *The Endless Summer* surf movie on the dull yellow plaster wall above my bed and leafed through a copy of *Surfer* magazine, all while keeping an eye on Chip. We each had our own desks, ancient and inscribed with initials carved by previous occupants. The desks were substantial, portending a heavy homework load. Each sat beneath lead-paned casement-mullioned windows that looked out toward the school's main entrance.

The room was small and spartan. One old cast-iron radiator, two dresser drawers, one mirror, one overhead light and wooden floors that looked as old and worn as the desks. The view offered the only hint of freedom but from five stories up, with the crowns of trees in the distance, the sun setting toward California behind them, the view felt less like an inspiration and more like a little jab to the heart. The room looked depressingly well-suited for two activities: study and sleep.

Chip had put on a pair of hand-tooled moccasins (sans socks) that he'd made in summer camp. Above his bed he taped a poster of a little girl standing in a field of wildflowers with the words "War Is Not Healthy for Children and Other Living Things." He hummed as he made his bed, laid out his toiletries and organized his dresser drawers while I lay stewing on my bed, itching to pull out my guitar and play "A Well Respected Man" by the Kinks. It was one of the few songs I could play all the way through and it summed up what I thought about prep school so far. A bell sounded and Chip looked up its meaning in the student handbook. It was dinnertime.

Dinner featured steak. It was a little tough and gristly, but steak nonetheless. It got my hopes up that the food would be better than at home but that was the last real steak we would see for a long time. Standard fare in the months to follow was Salisbury steak, which students referred to as elephant scabs, and chipped beef on toast, better known as shit-on-a-shingle. Several weeks later I was sitting in one of the fourth-floor communal bathroom stalls and saw a line of graffiti on the stall door that read "Flush twice, it's a long way to the kitchen." In all honesty, the fare at Taft might not have been fine cuisine but it wasn't tripe — a word my grandfather often used to describe something he didn't like. Another strange word he used was "bebop" — which is what he called the music I played on guitar. Based on the way he said it, it was on a par with tripe.

I don't remember exactly what I was doing that first night before mandatory lights out at ten. More than likely, I sat on my bed and played guitar or leafed through my *Surfer* magazine as the last grains of summer slipped through the hourglass. I was anxious about the first day of classes and whether I would fit in academically, athletically or socially.

At 10 p.m. sharp one of us switched off the ceiling light. Except for a small sliver of the hall light beneath our door, our room was completely dark. It had been a long day. I was tired, depressed and churning butterflies. Chip said he was going out for lower school football, which gave me confidence about making the team, but the way he'd organized his desk had me concerned on the academic front.

A breeze came through one of the casement windows. As my eyes were adjusting to the dark, I could make out one of the curtains billowing inward. The air in our room freshened, as it does just before a rain and then it did begin to rain. I only knew that by the sound of it pattering on one of the desks. I'd always liked a good rainstorm when we lived in Middlebury, especially ones with thunder and lightning, but this was a light, gentle rain. It did not inform what was about to come.

At first, I found it soothing and then something about it started to annoy me. I was sure Chip had opened the window on my side when I wasn't paying attention because he'd mentioned earlier that he "liked fresh air" at night — and now my desk was getting wet as a result of his indoor air quality requirements. I got up and closed the window. A minute later I heard Chip open it again.

I'd never shared a bedroom before, and I was starting not to like it. As I lay there wondering how to respond, it boiled down to two choices. I could either stay in bed and let Chip get the better of me, or I could do something about it. I got up, switched on the light to prove that rain was indeed landing on my desk and closed the window. Chip got up, telling me he needed fresh air for a good night's sleep. We stood toe-to-toe in the middle of the room and the tension that had festered between us all afternoon graduated into a full-blown argument.

We were at the point of push comes to shove when the sound of heavy footsteps pounding up the stairs made us stop, snap off the light and jump back into our beds.

Mr. Marx burst in. He started out by saying he could hear us all the way down on the fourth floor. Only he wasn't talking so much as yelling. Our pretending to be asleep only made matters worse. He told us we'd awakened the whole school. I found that hard to believe and had to bite my lip to keep from giggling since his decibel level was several orders of magnitude above what ours had been. He was making waking up the "whole school" and possibly all of Watertown if he kept it up. During a short pause in his tirade, one of us may have tried to squeak out an explanation. If so, he immediately cut it off. He was not interested in our excuses. He was there to teach us a lesson about the consequences of breaking the rules. Things were about to go from comical to serious.

Mr. Marx then methodically laid into each of us. He went after Chip first, standing over his bed, belittling him with taunts and insults that were crude and personal. Like Sgt. Carter chewing out Gomer Pyle — only uncensored and without the laugh track. As I listened, I wondered if this was normal teacher behavior at Taft. *Mr. Marx had just met our parents that afternoon.* I was hoping he would remember that at some point. Take a pause, realize he'd lost the handle, recognize that we were now scared, and calm down. I kept thinking that it was not too late to right himself. It was understandable. Everyone feels some stress at the start of a new school year. Why should teachers be any different? Chip and I would apologize to Mr. Marx and then to each other. Then we could all get some sleep and forget the whole strange, embarrassing incident.

Then with two quick strides, he was standing over me. I was next. I closed my eyes. I was scared. I could hear him panting, catching his breath as he decided what to do with me. I didn't know what to do other than play possum and pretend to be asleep.

He lingered there for half a minute without saying a word. That told me he had something worse in store for me than a verbal dressing down and I sensed something bad was about to happen. "And *you!*" he shrieked. He then struck me across the face with a hard, open-handed slap. I did not move. My eyes were locked tight and remained that way after he switched off the light and slammed the door shut. I was in shock, rigid with fear, unable to move. Afraid he might fly back in at any moment in a bigger rage and hit me again.

I was in uncharted waters. I'd never been hit by an adult before. The side of my face stung. Time passed slowly. I listened for him out in the hall. If he returned, I told myself I would get up and defend myself. After the threat of him returning had passed, I stopped hyperventilating. My mind was busy processing what happened when I heard a muffled sound. It took a few moments before I realized Chip was whimpering.

I could not believe it. *I* got hit and *Chipper* was the one sobbing. All because of his priggish insistence for fresh air. Part of me didn't blame him. In all honesty, part of me felt like having a good cry too, but for different reasons. Unlike Chip, I did not want to be there, and this proved that my intuition about prep school was right all along. It felt nice to be right for a change. I only wished my parents were there to see it. I thought back to how bad it felt to be bullied when I first moved to Los Angeles. Before I learned how to stand up for myself and fight back. Compared to other boys my age, I was slim and doe eyed. Appearance-wise, I could pass for an adolescent girl. That, however, was not how I saw myself. I saw myself as athletic, rebellious, tough and attractive *to* girls. I wasn't going to accept getting smacked around in an all-boys school, where I already felt vulnerable and didn't belong. Especially by one of its teachers, no matter how venerable the school or its reputation. I realized then and there that, more than just wanting to, I *needed* to get revenge for what Mr. Marx had done to me. His slap was a confusing and disturbing wake-up call. My self-respect was under assault in an institution that was supposedly there to build it up.

I remained awake long after Chip cried himself to sleep. My mind swirled with anger toward my parents while replaying what had happened to make sure I hadn't missed anything to justify Mr. Marx's reaction — interspersed with fantasies of beating him to a bloody pulp.

I gave serious consideration to running away that night. It seemed like the logical thing to do after considering the circumstances. I was leaning toward hitchhiking back to California and show-ing up at my best friend Preston Iverson's house and asking for asylum. In many ways I felt closer to his parents than my own and I knew they would be sympathetic. But even if I made it there (which I was confident I could), his parents would call mine and then there would be a different kind of hell to pay. I had run away a couple of times in Los Angeles when I was new there, and it never got me anywhere or led to anything except a lecture for the worry I'd caused.

Several times that night, the urge to flee had me on the brink of getting out of bed. And then I would stop and think about the rumors that would spread around Taft the next day. Rumors that I was a homesick little rabbit who couldn't handle one night in a prep school. All my old friends from Middlebury would hear about it, and what would they think of me then? There was also the huge embarrassment it would cause my parents and grand-parents. I'd be facing their wrath and trying to live that down for years.

My parents had told me Taft was a liberal school, staffed with young, hand-picked, highly dedicated teachers who would provide a superior education. And here I was getting screamed at and hit in the face by one of them on my first night. It didn't add up. Were they setting me up and lying to me all along? Did they sell Taft as "liberal," knowing once I was in, there was no getting out until I "straightened up?"

I knew Mr. Marx did not exist in a vacuum. He was there because he presumably fit the mold the school wanted. When I finally did drift off to an uneasy sleep, I was left with two big questions: Was this normal teacher behavior at Taft? If so, how was I going to get myself out of it without ruining my reputation and putting my future at risk?

I woke up the next morning and checked my face in the mirror. I was hoping for a bruised cheek or shiner or any kind of badge that someone might ask about so I could get what happened out into the open. I was angry but also curious if any other lower mids went through the same opening night "orientation" that I did. Anyone, that is, except Chip. I could not get it out of my head that he was responsible and I got the worst of it. But there was no mark on my face and therefore no story to tell. Chip hummed as he dressed, as though nothing had happened.

CHAPTER 6

My first recitation after breakfast was history with Mr. Wynne. Mr. Wynne was the varsity wrestling coach, and had the squat, barrel-chested build of a former wrestler. He looked about Mr. Marx's age — early to mid-thirties — and he had an easy-going manner. That gave me hope that perhaps not all masters were going to be as harsh as Mr. Marx. There were twelve to fifteen of us, all wearing mandatory school-approved khaki trousers, wingtips (or loafers), shirts, ties and sport coats. Mr. Wynne outlined his curriculum for the fall semester and handed out textbooks. They were not the recycled public-school textbooks I was used to, but brand-new Time-Life hardbound books like the ones that graced my grandparents' bookshelves. First up was *Mesopotamia: The Cradle of Civilization*. We were given yellow Marks-A-Lot pens and encouraged to highlight key passages. That seemed extravagant and bordering on vandalism but I kept my thoughts to myself.

Between my lack of sleep the night before, the subject matter and the buzz from the fluorescent lights overhead, I became sleepy. I dozed off until the sound of laughter woke me. I opened my eyes and noticed I'd grown a pair of yellow tusks. Two pencils were hanging out of my nostrils. Mr. Wynne had inserted them while I slept, to everyone's amusement, including mine.

My second class was Latin. Growing up, my sisters would revert to pig Latin whenever they didn't want me to understand what they were saying. I therefore had a natural dislike along with a proven ineptitude for Latin. My mother told me that Latin would help me understand the root meaning of words. I already had a dictionary, so learning definitions through the roots of a dead language sounded like a thrill for another lifetime. But to under-score how seriously Latin and the classics were taken at Taft, our master was none other than the dean of students, Mr. Oscarson. "Oscie," as he was fondly referred to by everyone at Taft, looked half Tweedledum — the way his pants were hitched halfway up his immense girth — and half goon from a 1930s gangster movie with slicked-back hair and the contented look of a cat guarding an aviary. I had no problem staying awake in his class while he slowly walked up and down the aisles of bolted desks with his hands behind his back as if concealing a truncheon. I held my breath as he passed by my position, wondering if Mr. Marx had said something to him about me.

We opened our textbooks and were instructed to read the first sentence, which was, if memory serves: "*Gaul est en Gaulum.*" Mr. Oscarson asked for volunteers to translate. Swallowing hard and sweating bullets, I slowly raised my hand. "Mr. Coe!" he said after finding my name on the seating chart. "Gaul is in Gaul," I peeped, instantly regretting it when I saw the look on his face. "Anyone

else?" There were no takers. He ended the mystery with feathers practically coming out of his mouth: "*Gaul is in* France, *Mr. Coe!*"

A few weeks later, Mr. Oscarson announced that two students who had occasionally substituted when his duties required him

Dean of students Donald "Oscie" Oscarson

elsewhere would be taking over full time. And with that, Tom Gross and Jim Reed became our full-time Latin instructors. Our first close encounters with senior classmen. Teaching on alternate days, both were earnest at first, and then after a few weeks the wisecracks appeared. Gross would show up five minutes late, appearing disheveled from lack of sleep, his tie knotted at half-mast. He'd respond to wrong answers with retorts like "thou *art'st* a dumb cluck." Reed's putdowns were equally entertaining and usually pantomimed. Wrong answers seemed to befuddle his brain, producing pleasant foggy side effects that grew into cosmically helpless facial expressions. They were both united in squeezing the maximum amount of pleasure they could get out of teaching Latin to a room full of lower mid dimwits.

Some of the higher-achieving lower mids grumbled they were getting instructionally shortchanged, and that their next level Latin courses would be harder because of Gross and Reed's antics. I liked them both, but they did make me wonder. Latin was a subject they were obviously good at, yet they were far more interested in cracking jokes than teaching. Their class would turn out to be our lower mid introduction to BFD — the underground senior movement/philosophy at Taft that prescribed a large dose of cynicism as the only way to survive. Near the end of the school year, when admissions to colleges and universities became the focus, Gross and Reed's approach to Latin would finally make sense to me — if you can call it that. They recognized the waste of time spent learning one of Taft's more arcane subjects for what it was: a meaningless but necessary hoop to jump through.

Except for science class, the rest of our lower mid classes were held in the basement. In some classrooms, like Mr. Wynne's, there were no windows. In others, like Latin, the windows were at the same level as the lawns outdoors, which was where my eyes would wander and my mind would follow. Mr. Kusterer taught lower mid English in another subterranean bunker where we alternated between studying the *Elements of Style*, poetry, and novels like *A Separate Peace*. Mr. Kusterer was a young bachelor, maybe 30, with a wry expression. I always liked English — certainly more than Latin or foreign languages. Even I knew better than to pretend I would ever speak or understand another language as well as a native, so why bother? Other than limericks or something by Ogden Nash, I did not cotton to poetry either. Haikus and iambic pentameters had way too many rules and most poems we dissected were morose, angry or indecipherable. Spare the flowery prose and give me:

Shake and shake the ketchup bottle
None'll come and then a lot'll.

I got upset with Mr. Kusterer once when he asked to us spell "PhD" on a "jap quiz." I'd never heard of a "Jap quiz" before Taft, but it aptly described a test or quiz you didn't know was coming. The term also was the closest we'd come to touching on modern history but that is probably beside the point. A PhD was undoubtedly something Mr. Kusterer was pining for but I thought it unfair of him to dock us for not knowing how to spell it and I let him know it after class. He cut me no slack, but all in all I liked his class and respected him for not teaching down to us. I also got the impression he did not see Taft as a permanent career, which made our classroom discussions less rote.

After lunch it was math and science. I can't remember who my math teacher was. Beyond the basics of addition, subtraction, multiplication and division, I wasn't all that interested in math. Knowing what something cost compared to how much money I had in my pocket was good enough for me. I had a lemonade stand's understanding of math in particular and economics in general. This made it hard for me to reconcile the fact that while public schools were "free" (paid for by property taxes), the cost of Taft was an added expense that came right off our family's bottom line. I could only surmise that sending me to a private school was for other reasons, because it made no sense from an economic point of view.

Geometry, algebra and trigonometry were the three big hurdles to jump through in high school math, with calculus the crowning achievement. I never did get acquainted with the last two and a large part of my frustration with math was rarely did teachers tie what we were learning back to everyday life. At Taft it was more of the same, though some devilishly practical applications did appear on tests — often along the lines of questions like this: Mrs. Fletcher sent her husband to the grocery store with a list of vegetables she wanted for dinner that evening along with $13.95. When he got to the store, Mr. Fletcher saw that turnips were $.87 a pound, radishes $.39 a pound, potatoes $1.15 a pound, broccoli $.47 a pound and yams $1.16 a pound. Mr. Fletcher wanted to see a movie that afternoon that would cost $3.50. Mrs. Fletcher instructed her husband to buy at least five pounds of yams because she liked yams. How many pounds of each vegetable would Mr. Fletcher have to purchase to end up with exactly $3.50 when he left the store? Try that with the clock ticking and cold sweat trickling from your armpits. My answer would have been, he should have married someone else, but that was not the answer teachers were looking for. Whether we were learning how to solve for x or y or both x and y, dividing or multiplying fractions, or determining when two trains were going to pass each other or collide head-on — it was all about remembering equations long enough to pass the quiz, test or final exam, and then dumping them from the memory bank to make room for the next set of formulas to memorize and regurgitate.

Math and science classes were held in the science building at the back of the main campus behind the pond. Those classrooms were newer, with plenty of windows and cheerful outdoor light, accessed by a walk outdoors around the pond over a pleasant, arching bridge. The science building had a futuristic-looking dome with a large telescope, and I'm sure most prospective parents were escorted through the new science building when considering Taft — rather than the basement dungeon where most of our lower mid classes took place.

My last class of the day was science, taught by Al Reiff. He looked to be 35 to 40 years old and wore a white lab coat over his suit, which lent him an air of authenticity. What he lacked in stature he made up for with his passion for science and gift for teaching. We started out by dissecting frogs. I suppose the one and only advantage of an all-boys school was that there might have been a little less high-pitched squealing when our scalpels pierced the frogs' soft white underbellies, but honestly not by much. We observed wriggling paramecium under microscopes, grew bacteria in Petrie dishes and learned about cell division and osmosis. Mr. Reiff had a scientific crush on Crick and Watson and he taught DNA, RNA and the double helix with the fiery conviction of a faith healer. The second half of our fall term we learned how photosynthesis occurred on the molecular level and how leaves turned CO_2 into O_2. Recognizing that plants were doing more for the planet and had more purpose in life than I currently did made me appreciate the formulas we learned enough to test well. Some of that had to do with the fact we were learning something rooted in the real world, as opposed to Latin, Mesopotamia, and ancient Greece, but to me Mr. Reiff stood out as an unusually good teacher at Taft, someone who showed a genuine passion for his subject.

Taft used a carrot and stick approach to keep lower school students academically keen. The carrot was the honor roll board in the main corridor. The stick was mandatory evening study hall. In addition, students were encouraged to enhance their class standing with any number of extracurricular activities from sports to theater to tutoring under-privileged kids from Waterbury. The race among lower mids to get off to a good start was especially fierce at the beginning of the year. We all wanted to make the honor roll or, if not that, achieve other forms of success so we could report them back home. Proud parents tend to be more loving and supportive, while disappointed ones were left with "try harder." This dynamic was magnified at Taft. As the masters took over the role of our parents, the natural desire to please, and receive praise in return, shifted from our parents to them.

With any trust I might have had gone after that first night, I avoided Mr. Marx and other masters. I stuck to my studies without brown-nosing or asking for help. I had only my previous junior high to compare with Taft, so I was surprised and disappointed that while my former school offered vocational courses for boys who might eventually prefer to work with their hands as well their brains, Taft offered no such courses. Except for Mr. Reiff, I don't remember any of my lower mid teachers linking what we were studying to modern-day jobs or current events.

With its own barber shop, student store, infirmary and hamburger stand known as the "jigger" shop — there was no reason to leave Taft's premises. That was backed by this warning in the student handbook: "In order to avoid possible incidents with town youngsters, students are requested not to sit on the front fence of the school nor loiter around that area." Further summing up our privileged segregation from Watertown's public-school ruffians was Taft's alma mater, which we were prompted to sing at vespers. The first two stanzas went like this:

> *O kind firm molder of a thousand boys*
> *Mother of destiny, dear, lovely place,*
> *Where glamorous beauty dwells and unguessed joys*
> *Give work and play an unsuspected grace.*
>
> *How like a little city, beauty clad,*
> *You stand in ivied loveliness and charm;*
> *Beholding you, the student's heart is glad;*
> *He goes secure to your enfolding arm.*

I guess it went without saying that Taft's alma mater made no mention of the benefits of corporal punishment. Our isolated "little city" would only become smaller and more magnified over time, until it was the world outside of Taft that would begin to seem strange.

CHAPTER 7

The moment I'd been preparing for all summer finally arrived. Class was over at 1:41 p.m. and "Athletics" were scheduled from 2:15 to 4:15. On that front, Taft had my old junior high school beat. I thought two hours of physical education was very forward thinking. After shedding my school uniform, I headed to the basement in blue jeans and sneakers. I was ready to play football and get some exercise to help clear my mind. Instead, I found myself stuck in a human traffic jam, standing at the end of a very long line to get my jersey. Inching forward, I had time to study the faces in the photos of every Taft team in every sport dating to the late 1800s. They lined the cinderblock walls. I suppose the purpose was to remind us that there was a rich athletic history at Taft, but all I could focus on was the change in haircuts and uniforms over the years, and the boys' faces that ranged from dull-witted, handsome, tough and determined to goofy looking. Many of them had haircuts that reminded me of Alfalfa in *Our Gang*. By the time I got up to the counter a good forty-five minutes later, my enthusiasm was dulled by the imprint of a thousand Taft student athletes dead and buried.

The man who ran the school store where we purchased our green banker lamps and desk blotters at the beginning of the year was handing out the football gear. Joe Lakovitch, with his white crew-cut and a bandy-legged gait, was a cross between a Schnauzer and a junkyard dog. What he lacked in height he made up for with a nasty bark — especially if you wavered or questioned whatever he was selling or handing out. He was a fixture at Taft, beloved by some of the older students for his crusty demeanor and feared by lower mids like me for his salty pugnacity and short fuse.

By the time I got up to the wizard of togs, I felt a little less confident about my impending football career. Roommate Chip was in line but so were sixty to seventy other boys. I bought a pair of used cleats from an older boy so I didn't have to shell out for those. It seemed like a veteran move, even if they did smell like dried steer manure. After stealing a few glimpses and getting some unasked-for but necessary help from an assistant coach, Mr. Williams, I was finally all suited up in my first fully padded football jersey. I gingerly made my way across the slippery concrete floor and out into the open air and fresh cut grass, feeling rather invincible with all my padding. I was ready to butt heads and prove how tough I was.

Our head coach was Mr. Leonard Sargent — one of three masters on the fourth floor HTD (for Horace Dutton Taft) with an apartment directly below Mr. Marx's. I assumed he'd heard Mr. Marx roaring up the stairs the first night. I hoped what happened hadn't been reported to him. Sarge's face was weather-beaten in a rugged, handsome way, and with his pipe and Irish Setter, he reminded me of Gil Favor, the experienced and level-headed trail boss on the TV show *Rawhide*.

He quietly confessed about Taft's mediocre lower school record on the gridiron the year before as if he were partly to blame. A spontaneous murmur rose up among us that we would not let him down. We would never again be so united, and by the time he finished his pep talk, to a man we were ready to give him an undefeated season.

After some calisthenics to loosen up followed by several punishing rounds of push-ups and sit-ups in the sapping mid-afternoon heat and humidity, topped off by several laps around the practice field, we were finally allowed to scrimmage. I got the call to go in on defense on the last set of downs. Morgan Werner, a middler

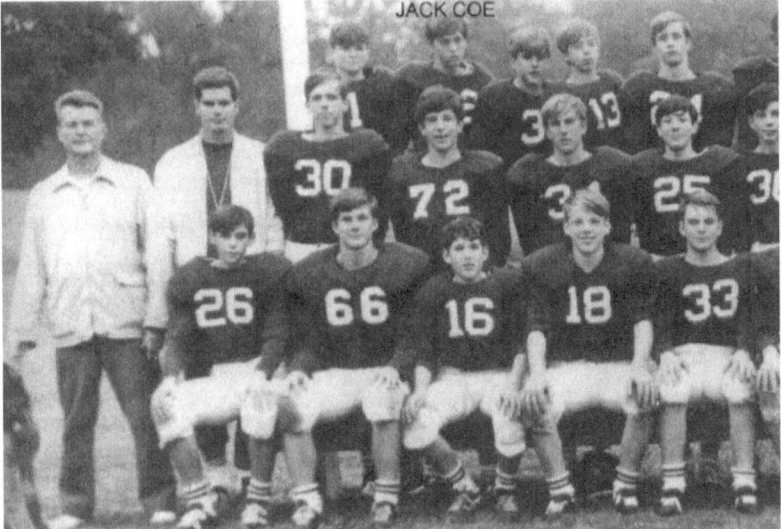

Coaches Leonard Sargent and Mr. Williams with the lower division football team, fall 1968. I'm in the back row, second from the left.

who was projected to be the starting quarterback, threw a Hail Mary pass on the last play and I intercepted it, running a few confused yards before I was knocked to the ground and piled on. I was walking on air when I left the field, certain that my interception would vault me to the front of the lower mid receiving corps and perhaps even bump me up to the junior varsity squad. As it turned out, I had a lot to learn about Taft athletics and even more to learn about myself.

In no time at all I found that free time at Taft was an oxymoron and one idled leisurely at one's own peril as others studied harder to get ahead of you. After Saturday classes ended at one in the afternoon, there was the rest of Saturday and Sunday to catch up on homework, cheer on the varsity soccer or football teams if they were playing at home, or go socialize in the lower mid common room, which was up the last flight of stairs above the Tower. The common room had a couple of sofas and two ping pong tables. Off that were two smaller rooms, one with a black and white television and the other with a record player. On Sunday mornings after breakfast, the jocks would crowd in to watch whatever pro football games were on. During one game, a car commercial came on with a house that looked very familiar to me. When I blurted out, "Hey, that's my old house!" several boys looked at me in disbelief, like I had to be lying to draw attention to myself.

While I was busy trying to establish myself as the alpha male over Chip, there was a broader move to establish the pecking order within the lower mid class. That took place on the fourth floor where the rest of the lower mids lived. After dinner on my first or second Saturday night, I ventured down to the fourth floor to get the lay of the land and a handle on my classmates.

Coming from a laid-back beach town in west Los Angeles in the late 1960s to a tightly controlled and competitive school like Taft, I not only didn't fit in — I didn't really want to fit in. With its long list of rules, Taft seemed repressive and socially backward. I was hoping to find some classmates who felt the same way.

In one room I wandered into, four or five boys were taking turns lighting farts, with little blue flames shooting out between their bare butt cheeks. In another room, monster magazines with black and white photographs from movies like *The Wolf Man*, *Dracula* and *Frankenstein* were being compared and discussed. A few boys were in the corridor playing hockey. In other rooms I peered into, boys were quietly studying to get ahead on next week's assignments.

There was only one other lower mid from California, John Dant. John lived on the fourth-floor landing next to Mr. Sargent's apartment. When I ducked into his room one Saturday afternoon, he was dozing on his cot wearing a pair of black eyeshades. John was from San Francisco and was a very cool cat. He played a blues harp, wore desert boots and was tuned into the Northern California music scene and the San Francisco underground. He and his roommate, Lee Penn, had a record player in their room and one of the first things John did was spin the first Led Zeppelin album for me. Lee was a quiet local Connecticut boy and his parents would bring him a box of crullers on weekends. I made it a point to stop by and beg for one every Saturday, mostly as an excuse to visit with John. In terms of what was hip and what wasn't, John was light years ahead of everyone in our lower mid class. In October John built a small still in his room and began fermenting apple juice obtained from a farm stand near Watertown. How he managed to get away with all this under the noses of the senior hall monitors and Mr. Sargent was a mystery. It was my first exposure to the underground culture at Taft and how some students got around the rules.

John Dant and I quickly became eligible for study hall and sat across from each other. Study hall was held in a large room above the dining room between 7 and 8 p.m. There was row upon row of bolted wooden desks, maybe 250 in all, with fluorescent lights overhead. The proctor sat at a desk off to one side and laid out the rules. There was to be no talking, whispering or passing notes. Someone made the mistake of testing him the first night

Evening study hall

and received a fierce tongue-lashing. That proctor, and the main study hall proctor that year, was none other than Joe Lakovitch, the wizard of togs and student supply commissar. Study hall proctor was the perfect job for him. A place to take out his anger on boys who seemed to have privileges he never had. John eventually handed me a note when Mr. Lakovitch wasn't looking. It read "Toke up? Hell yes!" I didn't even know what that meant. A few minutes later I handed him this less than sensical folded response: "Whomp shit-ass motherfucker." It kind of underscored the difference between growing up in LA and San Francisco, but we were now two foreigners in a strange land. That would lead to a mutual West Coast bond and eventually a friendship before we'd ultimately go in different directions.

The cliques that took shape early in our lower middle class were not so different than those at my old elementary and junior high schools. The most popular boys were the best athletes. Nick Lo Russo was the only lower mid to make the varsity football team, but instead of making him the leader of our class, this almost had the opposite effect. He was nice, friendly and humble, but a physical man-child compared to the rest of us. Varsity football practice ran longer than ours and he would sometimes be trudging wearily up the steps as the rest of us were heading down to vespers. The expectation that he would be Taft's star tight end the following year seemed to weigh on him. While the rest of us were there to learn and ostensibly enjoy the journey, he was there primarily to do the job he was recruited for. Combined, these things set him apart.

Lower mids who made the junior varsity squads in football and soccer formed the core of our seven-member class committee.

Class committees met in private with faculty advisers to decide, among other things, the fate of classmates who were caught cheating or breaking other rules. Our class committee leader was Peter Miller, a jovial sandy-haired JV football player with an outsized personality. Peter's spot-on Elvis Presley imitation cemented his status as the lion king of our class.

The brains of our class quickly established themselves. Erik Kitchen and Bruce Braine led the pack with a one-two punch. They were not as popular as the jocks but they were not looked down on either because of the emphasis Taft placed on academics. In the main hall that every student passed by several times a day was the prominently displayed honor roll board that listed the current rankings of the highest academic achievers in each class. Later in the year, when I was regularly breaking out of my room late at night, I made the honor board by removing the glass pane and rearranging the letters to spell my name — earning a "grade" (demerit) for my effort.

There were a few lower mids who had older brothers at Taft. They seemed to know what to expect and settled in quickly. There were several boys whose fathers or grandfathers had attended Taft. In those cases, some of the masters and administrators knew who they were, either by their last names or their family's support of the school through endowments and gifts. You might think that the perks of being a legacy student would lead to snobbery or favoritism. If so, it was not obvious. Whatever our circumstances were when we entered Taft, in the beginning we were all in the same boat when it came to competing in class and on the athletic fields, while also learning how to get along.

There were three additional lower mids besides John Dant who I thought might be worth knowing. One was Richard Bixby. There was a rumor he had a Gibson Hummingbird electric guitar under his bed that he guarded like it was gold. One Saturday afternoon, word got out that he was playing it and I went down to see for myself. He was sitting on his cot trying to play "Suzie Q" with Creedence Clearwater's album beside him. Several boys were milling about, trying to get a glimpse of the sacred instrument. Eventually I squeezed my way inside the room and worked up the courage to ask if I could play it. He was a louche southerner from Savannah, Georgia, and his immediate reaction was to put the guitar back in its velvet-lined case, slide it back under his bed, and shoo me away.

Another boy eyeing the guitar that day was Bruce Maclean. Bruce was from Waterbury. I remembered him as the cigarette king at the party I'd attended in Middlebury earlier that summer. He was in my history class with Mr. Wynne and reminded me of one of those Cupid cherubs on the eaves of old New York City buildings, ready to rain down mischief on the working stiffs below. He had the same mirthful scowl I remembered from the party, and given my rocky start at Taft, I thought we might have something in common. Bill Waldron, another student in our history class, was a lethal combination of funny, smart and good-looking. Without effort he became one of the most popular lower mids. Bill and Bruce hit it off, which made me jealous. I wanted Bruce to become a full-fledged malcontent like me, not hang out with someone like Waldron who had success written all over him.

Another lower mid who drew my attention was Chris Walcott. He was a clean-cut, good-looking black kid from New Haven with long eyelashes and a streetwise, laid-back manner. The first time I saw him, he was sauntering down the fourth-floor corridor with a long-handled comb stuck fast in his hair. Chris was far friendlier and more outgoing than my flatmate Willie Barley. I hardly ever saw or spoke to Willie. Willie kept his radiator valve wide open throughout the year. The few times he opened his door when I happened to be out in the hallway, I would be met with a blast of hot air mixed with the overwhelming scent of whatever cologne he happened to be crop-dusting with. He could often be heard singing "Cloud Nine" by the Temptations, as though trying to ward off the evil spirits. Taft isolated all incoming black students by putting them in single rooms, which sent a message that while Taft was progressive in its admissions policy, there was a reason, left for students to figure out, that blacks and whites shouldn't room together.

Early on, Bruce and I met in Chris's room one night after lights out. We opened the window, stuffed a towel under the door, sat on the edge of Chris's bed and tried smoking rolled up notebook paper. This was my idea, before Bruce came up with a steady supply of real cigarettes. It tasted more rancid than it sounds, and Bruce and Chris gave me a look that told me I should keep my dumb ideas to myself. After our burning throats recovered, we talked for a while. As Bruce and I were getting ready to leave, there was a knock on the door. The knob turned and Mr. Sargent poked his head in.

"What's going on here?" he asked, knowing full well he'd caught us red-handed. He looked pleasantly bewildered, as though a blind street urchin in a wheelchair just tried to pick his pocket. Bruce and I always prepared alibis when we went out catting after lights out. We said we were helping Chris with a homework assignment and lost track of time. He came in and started sniffing around. "I smell smoke. Do you smell smoke?" We all frowned and shook our heads, trying to convey that his pipe smoking senses were to blame and his suspicion was way beyond anything we would ever think of doing. He picked the towel off the floor and gave it a whiff. We told him it was there to keep our study session quiet, out of respect for our fellow students. Mr. Sargent let out a sigh of exasperation, ran his weathered hands through his hair and gave us all a stern warning before sending Bruce and me back to our rooms.

CHAPTER 8

Like most New England prep schools at that time, Taft was not a particularly religious school. Three times a year we had to go attend a church in Watertown across the green from the one I went to as a child. Taft had a chaplain, Mr. Zaeder, who occasionally spoke at vespers. Vespers was held before dinner every evening Monday through Friday in the Bingham Auditorium. Except for meals, it was the only time all the students and faculty gathered together. Vespers lasted fifteen to twenty minutes and student silence and attentiveness were enforced by masters who sat on the aisles with their grade books conspicuously tucked in their sports coat pockets. Mr. Esty, the headmaster, was the main speaker, with Mr. Zaeder sometimes introducing Mr. Esty after a short prayer and a word or two about how important belief in God was to our healthy development and well-being in an increasingly secular world. To polite applause, Mr. Esty would stride up to the podium and soak up the admiration before settling down his audience. Mr. Esty was a confident speaker. I would have related to him more if he told us something about his life and shared some personal stories about growing up when he was our age. But he never did that. Instead, his speeches were mostly seasoned with quotes from famous and not so famous philosophers and other historical figures. They usually led to, and ended, with Taft's mission statement and motto: *"Non ut sibi ministretur, sed ut ministret."* "Not to be served, but to serve." His message was always reinforcing his belief that attending Taft was a privilege, and we were fortunate to be there.

I remember only part of his first vespers speech and for good reason. When he addressed the lower mids directly and said, "A lot of our traditions at Taft may seem strange and new to you but in time you will learn to embrace them." Coming as it did the same week that Mr. Marx slapped me, I wondered if Mr. Esty was speaking directly to me. But was he offering me an olive

John Esty, headmaster

branch — or letting me know that what Mr. Marx had done was one of "Taft's strange and new traditions" that I would "get used to"? As I walked to dinner that evening, I half expected Mr. Esty to seek me out and offer a few private words of encouragement or maybe even an apology for what Mr. Marx had done. That would have made a world of difference in my attitude. As it was, he not only didn't, but in my two years I don't recall him ever speaking to me one-on-one. As for the "strange and new traditions," they were just getting started.

The main ways I could escape my insecurities, be myself, and not worry about the future were playing guitar or being outdoors. In New England there are the so-called Indian days of summer, where the air is warm and dry, just around the time the leaves start to turn and the lawns are still green. Little pop-up thunderstorms will sneak up some afternoons while on other days billowy white clouds sail east toward the Atlantic. The poets and poems we were studying in Mr. Kusterer's class all seemed to agree that being outdoors on a beautiful day was good for one's soul. To teach us that while preventing us from doing what those poems inspired had a sort of blind cruelty about it. Winter was just around the corner. With snow on the ground, there would be plenty of time to analyze Robert Frost's "A Swinger of Birches" without lamenting lost opportunities.

I began to gravitate to Bruce Maclean and Whit Gray's room on the fourth floor after football practice. Bruce's assessment that "Taft sucks" aligned with mine. Whit agreed. I would tell them how great California was and that would rile us up and we'd grouse about our lack of freedom at Taft. We'd talk about the war in Vietnam and other current events we knew very little about as we were now cut off from current events except for what we read in *Time* or *Newsweek*. Following in their fathers' footsteps, several students got the Sunday *New York Times* delivered to their doors, which they'd retrieve in their bathrobes and slippers like middle-aged apartment dwellers. Sections of the *Times* would wind up in the general population later in the day.

Most lower mids accepted the transition of authority from their parents to Taft as part of growing up. Many seemed to embrace it as a jumpstart into early adulthood. Bruce was the only other lower mid I knew who questioned the future that our parents and Taft were prepping us for. We did not want to become copies of our fathers. We wanted freedom, the kind you don't have when you're trapped in a room with a window that opens to the inaccessible outdoors. That yearning to be free and hold onto some

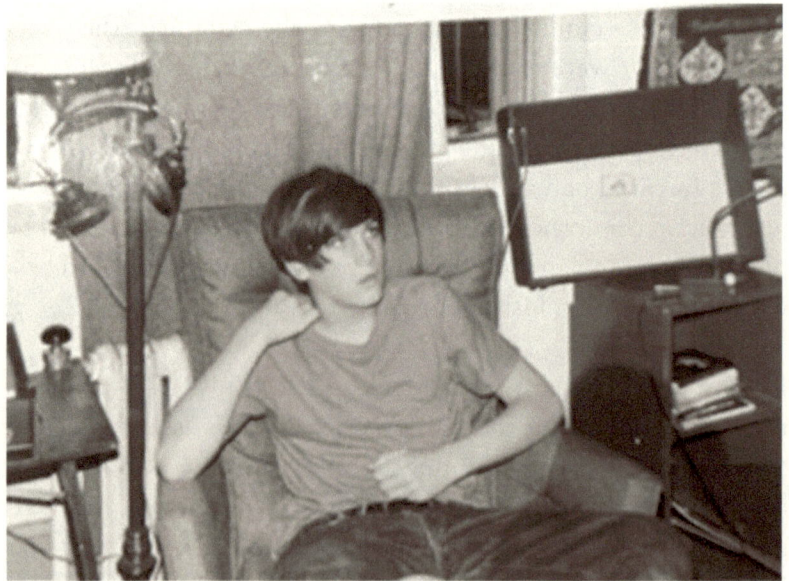

In Bruce's room

part our childhood led to this: If we couldn't leave our rooms at certain times of the day, we'd make something that could.

Made out of notebook paper, our paper airplanes all had names depending on how they performed in flight. The *Wop Trawler* was the simplest design. Very crude with a minimal number of creases, it back-flopped repeatedly until we added a paper clip for balance. It then sailed in a straight-line out Bruce's window toward the white split-rail fence, slow and steady, like the blimps my father flew on submarine patrol off the coast of San Francisco during World War II. The *Dipsy Doodler* was far more complex. With over a dozen folds including ailerons, it dipped, flipped and changed directions on a dime.

The helicopter didn't have a name but with its Y-shaped rotor blades, it could stay aloft for several minutes if the updrafts were good. Before long, the curious began to abandon their afternoon studies and crowd into Bruce's room for the afternoon paper airplane shows.

Senior monitors would carry out random spot checks to make sure we were studying quietly at our desks after athletics and before vespers. The worst was Rudy Shafer, who relished this cat and mouse game. He would take his shoes off and sneak up the Tower stairs after making his rounds on the fourth floor. Catching me listening to my transistor radio one afternoon, he confiscated it and wrote me up. When the opportunity presented itself, seniors and upper mids let lower mids know their place in the pecking order. There was "milk lunch," a mid-morning nutrition break between classes held in the basement where a select group of seniors handed out chocolate milk and donuts to some four hundred hungry students. In reality it was a rugby-style free-for-all where your size and ability to push and shove determined whether you came away empty-handed. That practice ended before anyone was trampled, but seniors and upper mids did not give up another Taft tradition called tray-dropping — where student waiters with fully loaded dinner trays would "accidentally" drop them ("oh my!") on the terra cotta floor. The dining room would go completely silent followed by a roar of approval from the students and stern looks from the masters, who were not amused.

There were three masters on the fourth floor, Mr. Sargent, Mr. Comiskey and Mr. Greene. They largely stayed in their apartments and left the lower mid corridor policing to the monitors. Once the mons had established a certain level of fear and order, they slacked off on the room checks, allowing the mice to play. And play we did as we were starving for fun. The focal point was Bruce and Whit's room, where after the launching of paper airplanes for the better part of an hour, pillow fights with squirt guns and water balloons would erupt and spill out into the hallway. As more lower mids joined in, Bruce and I realized we'd tapped a vein that undermined the school's authority and purpose. The good times went on for several weeks until the fourth-floor masters heard enough one day and ordered all of us back to our rooms under the threat of "bounds," meaning our permission to leave school on weekends would be revoked and we would be forced to do menial jobs on Sundays. Senior monitor patrols resumed with a vengeance after that.

The crackdown made my getting down to Bruce and Whit's room more difficult. Peering around corners for the senior monitor on duty and racing down the corridor when the coast was clear were like playing Capture the Flag or Kick the Can. I liked the thrill of outfoxing the mons and became good at not getting caught. But danger was always lurking.

I was in Bruce's room one afternoon and spied an open can of White Rock Cola. It seemed only fair that he should offer me a sip but I didn't want to come off as a total mooch. I was already bumming his cigarettes, and friendship only goes so far. I kept eyeing the can and its label with the attractive girl with the dragonfly wings resting on a rock in the middle of a stream, but still no offer from Bruce. By then I'd grown extremely thirsty and wanted something cold, bubbly and sweet, and so I did something to distract him and stole a quick gulp. It wasn't quite what I expected.

Bruce had started sneaking out of his room late at night, either to visit friends or smoke a butt in the stairwell. Getting wise to this, one of the mons on night watch had begun setting his own empty soda can on Bruce's outer doorknob. If Bruce turned the handle from the inside after lights out, the can would drop to the floor and alert the mon. This forced Bruce to relieve himself in his own can, which he hadn't gotten around to emptying that afternoon. The surveillance tactic was old news for Bruce, but it turned out to be bitter tasting news to me.

I liked the occasional cigarette. Every few months I'd steal one that my parents kept around for their dinner guests. It was a guilty pleasure that sometimes seduced me when I was stressed. It made me wonderfully lightheaded for a short time, and then I'd feel weak — believing it was a bad habit and a slippery slope to ruin. My parents had both quit smoking when I was young as its ill effects were just starting to become known. At Taft, smoking was so widespread among the upper mid and senior classmen that I'm surprised Taft didn't cash in and install cigarette machines. Cigs, coffee and NoDoz were all widely known aids for pulling "all-nighters" — the last night left for procrastinators to finish term papers or cram for final exams. "All-nighters" showed *commitment* and the masters all knew it. How a student achieved high honors in the classroom didn't matter to them — as long as cheating wasn't involved.

One of my first purchases was a hot coil to boil water to make instant coffee in my room. Lower mids and mids were not allowed to smoke, but upper mids and seniors had their own place to smoke, relax and unwind. The Wade House, a rustic cabin nestled among pine trees near the hockey rink, was a bohemian retreat where they could go watch television, listen to music and do pretty much whatever they wanted. It was one of the rewards for making it through the first two years at Taft.

If you were on a traveling sports team, it was against the rules to smoke or drink at home or at anyone else's home. Whether I would continue smoking on the sly and perhaps ruin my athletic career at Taft if I got caught was an issue. At times I felt strong, like after a football practice where I'd done something right and one of the coaches noticed. But on a team that was three positions deep and with several returning middlers who had seniority, my interception on the first day of scrimmage was quickly forgotten.

A middler named Andre Bell got the starting nod at split end, which I badly wanted. For me, there was nothing worse in football than being a lineman. That position was for the slow and plodding, like my roommate Chip, not for thin, fleet-footed athletes like me who could slip behind a defender on a stop-and-go route and make the overhead fingertip grab on the way to the end zone and glory. Despite my supreme confidence, or maybe because it rubbed some of the coaches and returning players the wrong way, I soon found myself battling for a position in the trenches. I would often line up against another lower mid named Ricky Rydzik, who was neither fat nor slow and often left me flat on my back. The assistant coach, Mr. Williams, would often use the two of us as examples of good fundamentals versus bad ones.

We were taught certain plays and would practice them in slow motion until we got it right. They had names like "23 Blast" that ran right up the gut for no reason that I could see. Every play was choreographed and, like learning a new dance step, this foot went here and that foot went there and your hips turned in this direction or that. After everyone learned their assignments for a particular play, we would practice them at quarter speed, half speed, three-quarter speed and finally at full speed — which was when things usually fell apart. Despite the mounting evidence, Mr. Sargent was supremely confident that if we executed our individual assignments to perfection, there was no reason every play we ran on offense shouldn't result in a touchdown.

The only enjoyable part of practice was when we earned a little time at the end to scrimmage. But that became less fun as cliques and rivalries developed over who the starters would be — especially between the returning mids and lower mids. Instead of coming together as a unit, by the time the regular season started we were at odds with each other more than we

were with opposing teams. In the communal shower after practice, middlers would stomp on a bar of soap and launch it like
a hockey puck into the groins of lower mids for sport. I sat on
the pines for most of our regular season games except for a few
plays at the end in garbage time. I have no recollection of any of
them except for one away game. There was a loud roar from the
field above ours where the JV team was playing. Word eventually
passed down from our student manager that Rick Wood, a fellow
lower mid, had completely whiffed the football during a kickoff.
I knew just how he felt.

"Feeds" were one of those Taft traditions that, in Mr. Esty's words,
were "strange and new" to me. Around the time rumors about
feeds filtered down to me, I received the formal invitation to
my first. Every student had his own post-office box — a small
gilt bronze box with a little window that brought the occasional
letter from the outside world. My invitation came from Mr. Marx.
He was my adviser — and also the adviser to Chip, Willie and
a handful of other lower mids on the fourth floor. I'd done a
good job avoiding Mr. Marx after the first night, but this was
a mandatory event. The purpose of a feed was to get to know
your adviser better over pizza and soft drinks in the relaxed,
informal setting of his apartment. As a bonus, a feed got you
out of regular dinner.

As my adviser, Mr. Marx was obligated to write my parents three
times a year to let them know how I was doing. He informed me
of this sometime in the fall semester and it was another reason for
me to avoid him. By then I was aware of his stature at Taft. No
master or student said a bad word about him to me or suggested
I avoid him. He wasn't considered strange. Quite the contrary,

in fact. Mr. Marx was the only master at Taft to have a "society" named after him, by students who worshipped his caustic wit and lofty demands in the classroom. Those who lived up to his expectations called themselves "Marxmen."

One evening not long before my "feed," several Marxmen arrived at his apartment for a feed of their own. They were dressed like Roman senators wearing flowing togas and head wreaths. One of them was Todd Gipstein, who was in his academic element at Taft. Mr. Marx called me out of my room in the middle of the soiree and grinned with delight as Todd rattled off all the US presidents' names in chronological order — first forward and then backwards — all in one impressive breath. It was one of Mr. Marx's early attempts to let me know that I was not up to Taft's academic standards. Over time he would tell me, sometimes impatiently and at other times sympathetically, that I was at Taft for "other reasons." leaving me to guess what those were.

My first feed at Mr. Marx's started shortly after I'd returned from football practice. There were ten or twelve boys crowded into his small apartment when I arrived. I stood eating pizza, talking to Mark Erickson from Upper Nyack, New York, until we proved we had nothing in common and moved on to our next victims.

Mr. Marx sat next to two or three boys on his couch, holding what looked like a conductor's baton. This was my first time in his apartment. I kept my distance while keeping an eye on him. He alternated between loud, sarcastic banter and listening to the Boston Pops with a rhapsodic appreciation for the music that he would occasionally "conduct" with his eyes closed. On the whole it was a pitiful affair. The late afternoon hues outside his window turned into one of those dreary old masters' paintings. I did my best to introduce myself and talk to as many of the other boys as I could, but preppy social graces did not come naturally to me. There were occasional squeals of laughter coming from the couch, but every time I glanced over, I'd missed the cause. We were finishing our cupcakes and the party was fizzling out when Mr. Marx suddenly got off the couch and took to the center of the room with a flourish. Wielding his baton like a sword, he began thrusting it into the crotch of any boy nearby. I couldn't believe what I was seeing. But the reaction to what he was doing amazed me even more. Spilling over the coffee table and chairs trying to evade him while pushing others in to "get goosed," the boys seemed to enjoy it — a spirited game of crotch tag by an unpretentious master who knew how silly boys could get — and should get — to relieve their pent-up anxieties and energy.

I made my way to the door as I watched it unfold. By the time Mr. Marx was finished, several exhausted students lay strewn across the floor and on the couch, laughing hysterically, while Mr. Marx held his baton aloft in the middle of the room, in a victory pose. He locked eyes with me and then said in a sarcastic voice, loud enough for everyone to hear, "Oh come on, Coe, don't be such a prude." I froze and the room became quiet as all eyes turned on me. It was a bit of genius on his part. With that one line he elevated himself as the pied piper of fun while branding me as the lone Pollyanna in the room.

After that, I had no doubt I was in a sick place and needed to escape. Once more I started thinking about my options. Running away was still a possibility, but I was in the same position as before. I did not know to whom or where to turn. My parents for sending me there? They obviously couldn't be trusted. I could go tell Mr. Esty about it, but what would he do as the head of such a school where things like that went on? I was fairly certain he would tell me I'd overreacted. That I simply didn't understand the close bonds between students and masters at Taft — either because I was too immature or overly sensitive. He would tell me that none of the other students there had brought up a similar complaint. And if Mr. Esty did speak to him, it would give Mr. Marx a motive to make my life miserable when Mr. Esty wasn't around to protect me. When it came to the pecking order between a revered master and a lower mid, I knew exactly where I ranked. I decided to bide my time until I could come up with a better plan.

He knew I didn't like him, but that didn't discourage Mr. Marx from coming into our room whenever he felt like it. His visits often took place before vespers. He would walk in without knocking and flop on my bed while I sat at my desk; or I would get off my bed to go sit at my desk as soon as he entered. He liked to needle and poke fun at Chip and me, which usually centered around our physical immaturity. He took great pleasure in teasing that we were either "prepubescent" or "pubescent." He was also interested in knowing whether our pubic hair was starting to grow in. He would space these comments and questions around more mundane ones like how we were doing in school. He asked questions my own father never had. But after hitting me and goosing half a dozen boys at his "feed" — were his questions of a personal nature really that outrageous in the scheme of things? As bewildering as this may sound, not really. We became accustomed to them. We'd received no instruction or guidance regarding teacher behavior. It was our behavior that was under the microscope — not theirs. So, Chip and I got used to Mr. Marx's probing as a quirk of his personality. I still didn't like Chip but we no longer openly argued or fought. We were just in separate camps. Chip was so determined to "make it" at Taft that he would never question Mr. Marx's authority, behavior or intent.

Mr. Marx understood that my struggle to hold onto my West Coast identity was more important to me than succeeding at Taft. When he really wanted to get under my skin, he would call me "Jack Coe from Greenwich, *Conn*," gleefully aware how much I hated Greenwich. Otherwise, he simply took to calling me "you" followed by "dip," "dipshit," "flamer" or "pube." When he was in a feisty mood, he would tickle me and occasionally grab at my crotch and say "gotcha." I would defend myself but I was no match for him physically. He was 6'4" and I was closer to 5'6" and 120 pounds, I'm guessing.

Chip usually looked on as a silent observer, rarely a participant. I think he was a little jealous of Mr. Marx's attention toward me. Out of the corner of my eye I'd see Chip smile whenever one of Mr. Marx's verbal jabs landed. But I was Mr. Marx's preferred foil in the Tower. He found little sport in teasing Chip and he ignored Willie Barley altogether. I was the one he'd goad and get a rise out of before we all went down for another uplifting vespers, reminding us that we were "there to serve." In case we'd forgotten.

I finally came up with an escape plan a few weeks after the "feed" in his apartment. Enough time had passed so that my parents couldn't say I hadn't given Taft a try. I decided to call and ask them to get me out. I knew they wouldn't be receptive because they wanted me to be there and had made the investment, so I had to wait for just the right moment. I wasn't sure I had the verbal skills to convince them I was at the end of my rope, but that's where I was.

Looking back, there is one mystery I still can't explain to myself, and that is why I chose to call my parents from Mr. Marx's apartment. There was a bank of phone booths in the basement. For some reason I didn't make that choice. Maybe I was afraid another student would overhear me, or maybe I wanted the poetic justice of doing it on Mr. Marx's dime. One afternoon when I was feeling particularly down in the dumps, I asked Mr. Marx if I could use his phone for a private call. To my surprise, he let me use the phone in his bedroom and even closed the door for some privacy.

My father answered. He told me that he and my mother were on their way out to a dinner party. I tried to steady my emotions but my voice became weak.

"You'll get used to it," my father replied. "You're just homesick."

I demanded he put my mother on. I could hear him sigh as he handed her the phone. I begged her to come get me. It was all I could do not to cry. After a long silence she replied, "Why? What's the matter? Tell me what's wrong."

I recognized her worn-down voice, the one she used when the burden of one more complaint was too much. I stammered. There were too many things to say, too many emotions to put into words, especially over the phone. I promised to tell her the reasons when I got home.

"Try," my mother pleaded, sounding as if she was on the verge of breaking down. But what she meant by "try" was to keep trying. At Taft. For her sake.

I don't know if Mr. Marx eavesdropped on the call. I don't remember if he had another phone in his living room or perhaps had put his ear to the door. I wouldn't be surprised. But I was so certain that my parents would rescue me that I wasn't particularly worried about what he heard. At the very least, he would have seen the dejected look on my face when I came out of his room and known that whatever the call was about, it hadn't gone my way. If I'd called from the phone bank in the basement or even from a phone booth in Watertown, the result would have been the same. My SOS was a total failure.

CHAPTER 9

I felt numb after that call. I'd always believed that my parents would protect me from real harm. Now I realized that was an illusion. It depressed me greatly at first. It was like losing the last parent-child bond. Then I realized something. I was on my own now. Free to make my own decisions and chart my own path without a care about what my parents thought or said — or the worry or guilt brought on by trying to please them and the fear of falling short. In essence, my mind flipped after that call. My parents were no longer my parents. And I felt a rejuvenating sense of power in that.

For most of the fall term, it was the stairwell smoking sessions that kept my spirits up. Bruce had a cigarette rolling machine that at Taft, for lower mids like us, was right up there with the cotton gin. Between the finest of floor-swept pipe tobacco Borkum Riff (with wooden ships and nautical maps on the pouch for our smoking adventures), Prince Albert "in a can" (jail and boarding school were synonymous by that point), or American-made

Winstons — we always had something other than notebook paper to smoke in the stairwells late at night.

After the call to my parents, I alternated between feeling strong at some times and adrift at others. While my newly found independence felt invigorating, I was still stuck in a place I knew was eating away at my self-esteem and testing my sanity. And I saw no way out. I'm competitive by nature. I didn't want to sabotage my future in spite of the challenges I was facing, so I continued to try hard in class and on the athletic field. Bruce's roommate Whit would often join us in the stairwell for a smoke. Sometimes Peter Byerly, another lower mid Bruce had befriended, would join us. Dick Ziegler, another lower mid, would occasionally meet us there, too. We were starting to bond over what we had in common, which was a healthy, growing dislike of Taft.

Our stairwell bull sessions would average about twenty to thirty minutes. I did not bring up Mr. Marx because he was a painfully personal embarrassment who underscored my own weakness. I wanted to appear braver and bolder than I was. I also considered him part of a much larger problem, which was the school itself. We would talk about a variety of things, most of them focused on school. In a walled-off environment like Taft, rumors have a way of incubating. I was used to older boys who liked to brag about girls and sex. But it was an eye opener to hear some of the stories we heard. Especially in a school that prided itself on gentlemanly behavior and refinement. The stories we heard about what went on in private boys' and girls' boarding schools put what I heard in public school to shame. I would tell you what some of these rumors and stories were, but I've no interest in passing on sick stories. Whether there was any truth to them, based on my experience in boarding school so far, they were hard to completely dismiss. We were Taft's youngest students but in one respect we considered ourselves wiser than most. Borrowing a line from the Beatles' "While My Guitar Gently Weeps," some at Taft were so inverted that they couldn't see how perverted they'd become. The stairwell sessions were what would pass for group therapy today. After crushing out the last cigarette and hiding the evidence, we'd plan the next one and call it a night.

Chip and I were barely on speaking terms. When we did talk, it usually ended with him asking me to "have some common decency." It would be fair to say I didn't show him any decency at all – common or otherwise. We had gotten off to a bad start and I still blamed him. The more I got to know Chip, the less I respected him. Chip saw Taft as "the kind, firm molder of a thousand boys." I have no idea how Mr. Marx fit into Chip's embrace of Taft, other than to say some see only what they want to see. We never did talk about that first night, or Mr. Marx.

Mr. Marx would occasionally goad Chip. Crimson cheeks meant Mr. Marx had struck a nerve, such as asking Chip what "base" he'd gotten to with a girl. Chip would protest that it wasn't his or anyone else's business. Mr. Marx would find this highly amusing and then go right on pressing for details. In our fathers' absence, Marx had a gift for drawing us out that, over time, made his probing seem normal. Why wouldn't we want to talk with him about sex? It was part of what made prep school so special. He was our floor master and adviser, but he was also a mentor and confidant. An open, more honest version of our fathers who, at this point after all, had entrusted him to raise us.

My grandmother Nannie would drive to Taft on Sunday after-noons to bring me her homemade coffee cake. I would meet her in front of the school. She would ask how I was doing and I would tell her I was doing fine. She would ask how I liked Taft and I would tell her I liked it very much. She would simper and smile and tell me how nice that was to hear and that she and my grandfather Bobby were *so pleased* that I was at Taft and getting along so well.

"Well, I suppose I should be getting back," she'd say. "Your grand-father and I are having dinner this evening with the Torrances." She'd hand over the cake, and I would give her the peck on the cheek she expected in return.

I always felt bad lying to my grandmother, but I'd learned my lesson. When I straight-up told her that I didn't like Taft the first time she came to visit, she played the same card my parents did. After one or maybe two attempts at being honest with her, it became much easier to simply tell her what she wanted to hear. Back in my room, I'd eat as much of the coffee cake as I could and even share some with Chip. Not because I wanted to, but because the only place to keep leftovers, or a second cake, was in Mr. Marx's refrigerator.

CHAPTER 10

The first big school holiday was Thanksgiving. I went home to Greenwich and my sisters flew in from California. I was not happy with my sisters for getting to stay in Los Angeles and I was less happy with my parents for abandoning me. My anger was feeding on my pride and my pride was feeding my anger. At that point I wasn't about to open up again as I did on the phone call, and tell them about Mr. Marx and Taft's overall strange environment. My family had made them my problem and I owned it now. If that turned me into my family's problem, it was their tough luck.

Our long absence from each other did not make our hearts grow fonder. My mother, especially, looked stressed, unhappy, and worn out. She had turned completely against the Vietnam War while my dad, like many World War II vets, still believed, or wanted to believe, that we were there for the right reasons. To help ease the economic strains of the war, when President Nixon took office in 1969, he froze prices on certain commodities, including copper. Setting Anaconda's price on copper was supposed to be my father's job in New York, so that rendered him essentially useless. That led to a lot of three martini lunches before taking the John Cheever express train home to Greenwich each night. That made my mother unhappier still and led to her ultimatum that if he didn't stop drinking, she would leave him. All of that was kept from me at the time.

My sisters were firmly planted in California. They had no intention of ever moving back to Connecticut and the pretentious mansion my parents were building on Quail Road. My middle sister, who never missed an opportunity to goad me (and vice versa), was especially snarky. Pointing out that I was going to be stuck in Greenwich for the rest of my life; giving her the upper hand in our sibling rivalry for years to come. Given the circumstances, the facade of spending a wonderful Thanksgiving with each other in our little rented yellow house in Greenwich was about to come tumbling down.

As we were all sitting down to Thanksgiving dinner, I started a slap fight with my mother. By slap fight I mean more pretend than actual slapping — more the art of quickness and the touching of an opponent's face rather than striking. It was like the slap fights Frank Catando used to force on me before the start of Miss Graves's class at Paul Revere — minus the actual contact. It was the release of pent-up angst and energy from being cooped up inside the house on a dreary New England day. My father told me to stop it at the same moment I noticed a tear on my mother's cheek. I was about to tell her I was sorry when my father gave me a good, hard open-handed whack across my face. I was now two for two at getting slapped by the father figures in my life. I apologized to my mother, went upstairs to my room and cried myself to sleep. If I thought I couldn't go any lower that Thanksgiving, a few nights later I saw my older sister walking down the hallway in a short nightie before bedtime and had bad thoughts. After that, I couldn't wait to get back to Taft and the devil I knew. By then I'm sure everyone in my family felt the same about me.

The first lower mid to drop out of our class was Frank Kelly. He was a fellow benchwarmer on the lower mid football team. Rumor was that he had an acute case of homesickness and his parents came and picked him up while the rest of us were in class. Whatever his reason for leaving, there was no official explanation. Once you were admitted, not cutting it at Taft was a sign of failure on the part of the student, not the school. And any student leaving the fold was subject to rumors.

When the pressures at Taft got too intense, all eyes would turn to Mr. Esty for relief. Rumors would swirl at dinner that he would call a holiday and after several days passed without an announcement, there would be electricity in the air. Finally, he would rise from his dining room chair, to growing applause, and say the magic word. The room would erupt. It meant no school the next day and we were all free to do whatever we wanted. Sounding great in theory, the reality was tempered by the fact most of us spent the "free day" catching up on homework and studying — not so different than any other Sunday.

When a hunger pang struck, I would have to cross the hall and ask Mr. Marx for a slice of my grandmother's coffee cake. He would take a refrigerator tax and I would sit at his small kitchen table eating while he ate his on the couch, petting his dog and feeding it spilled crumbs. With its open sores from scratching and sagging, bloodshot eyes, the dog was a wreck, and no amount of air freshener could hide the stench of poor Argus. Overweight and swaybacked, Argus had a hard time getting up on the couch but once he did Mr. Marx would lavish him with dog biscuits and love, burrowing his face into Argus's matted fur, cooing "Noon-noon" or "Noonie."

It was times like that, when Mr. Marx wasn't acting hyper, that I saw the other side of him. While it was still unsettling to see him nuzzle a dog and not care If he caught fleas or mange, he did manage to show a genuine love for the beast. Even though I'd already seen Alfred Hitchcock's movie *Psycho*, it never occurred to me that Mr. Marx might have, or was developing, a split personality like Anthony Perkins. I just chalked up whatever it was to "his moods," and over time learned when to avoid him.

I watched Walter Cronkite's CBS nightly news with him a few times. His reaction to the reporting from Vietnam was complete obliviousness. He had nothing to say about the war or the men about his own age who were fighting it. One evening after study hall, he invited me over to watch *Lord of the Flies*. The book was a favorite of mine. When it was over, he had nothing to say but I wondered if he noticed what I did: the irony of boarding-school boys' descent into madness was the opposite of what was taking place in the Tower at Taft. We needed to be rescued not by him but from him. He watched the movie as intently as I did. But I believe he saw it from a completely different point of view.

Mr. Marx had only one adult visitor I can recall. A woman about his age was up in the Tower one afternoon. They were having a conversation out in the hall that rapidly grew heated. Eavesdropping from my room, I got the impression she was a teacher from St. Margaret's or Westover, the two girls' boarding schools nearest to Taft. The girls were sometimes invited over to take his advanced Latin class or act in one of the school plays. He had said or done something to upset her and she stormed off.

Mr. Marx never mentioned his parents, relatives or friends. He was a loner even among his teaching peers, going out for walks around the school on weekends with Argus leading on leash. Outside of listening to the Boston Pops, he had no hobbies or interests that I could see. He was like a tightly wound spring, held together by his dog at one end and ancient Greece and Rome on the other.

Letters from my friends back in Los Angeles slowed to a trickle. Early on, Preston sent me the KHJ radio list of top 40 hits with Spirit's "I Got a Line on You" at number one. Looking at the list was like reading an obituary of all the new music I was missing. And then came a real one. One of my good friends, Raoul Jimenez, a strapping, sweet-natured kid from one of the only Mexican families left in Pacific Palisades, had punctured a lung playing flag football. It turned out he had lung cancer and a letter or two later he was gone.

Raoul had been a beer-can collector. The shelves in his room were lined with empties, from common brands to prized rarities. I had collected a few East Coast beer cans I'd found trolling the woods around Highfield Country Club earlier that summer and mailed them back to him. Starting out with marbles, army men and baseball cards when we were very young, our collection phase was peaking just before I left Los Angeles, with beer cans for Raoul, and beer signs for the rest of us.

I never got into collecting stamps or coins. Beer signs were another matter. Neon signs were a must for any self-respecting collector, but even more popular were the hypnotic Bouncing Miller signs, the blissful Moving Water Hamm's and the extremely rare and incomparable Starry Night Hamm's. If I'd had a Van Gogh or Monet hanging in my bedroom when I was 13, I'd have traded it straight up for a Starry Night Hamm's.

The idea of plastering my room with beer signs had been on my mind ever since I arrived at Taft. My parents had forbidden me to take any of my own from home — along with my favorite stuffed animal that a friend had given to me as a going away present. Culturally and as a statement of maturity and taste, beer signs would be a giant leap over anything I saw on the walls at Taft. Furthermore, there was nothing in the Taft Student Handbook that ruled them out.

The two most popular posters that adorned lower mid rooms at Taft were Raquel Welch in a fur bikini from the movie *One Million Years BC* and a girl wearing nothing except a cowboy hat with outlines drawn all over her body labeling her "parts" as various cuts of meat. Between the maddeningly gorgeous Raquel and the butcher's pinup, I was determined to put something on my wall that didn't reek of prep school desperation. I signed up Bruce and Whit to join me on a beer sign hunt one weekend.

Beer sign hunting in LA was going out with your friends on a Saturday or Sunday to work the bars. Walking into establishments we weren't old enough to enter was a tricky business. A simple "Do you have any extra beer signs?" got you nowhere. But to identify yourself as a Boy Scout on a scavenger hunt and one of the things your scoutmaster put on the list was a "beer sign" — delivered with a quizzical, helpless look — *that* caught bartenders so off guard that before you knew it, they were escorting you back to a storage room where there were "a few old signs somewhere," while the loaded patrons cheered you both on. And if by chance the bartender handed you a cheap cardboard sign, you'd point to an electric one and, with heartfelt apology, mumble something about earning more points for the lighted one in the corner.

We had to get formal "permissions" to leave Taft on weekends, which meant a written invitation to visit someone's house, in this case Bruce's parents. Forging permission slips at Taft amounted to scribbling a signature that no one could read and having it signed by a master who barely glanced at it. We caught a bus to downtown Waterbury, which was sure to have more bars than Watertown. It was a cold overcast afternoon and by the time we arrived it was drizzling but my spirits were high. I knew Waterbury would be virgin territory and that the odds of hearing a bartender tell us that another scout troop had cleaned him out the week before were slim. I planned to show Bruce and Whit the ropes and then we'd all go solo. It was difficult to split a beer sign three ways.

For whatever reason, be it the gloomy weather or the depressive atmosphere of the once-bustling industrial city, there was no goodwill to be had in any of the bars. We were run out of one after another, all before I finished the first sentence of my spiel. Bruce and Whit looked at me like I was out of my mind and

I looked at them as carriers of bad luck. They agreed to wait outside while I went into one final establishment to give it a last shot. This bar had a little nook, a place to hang raincoats or remove galoshes, and on the alcove wall I noticed a lighted sign. It was a lousy one by California standards but it was better than nothing. The beefy bartender cut me off as had all the others and told me to get out. On the way out, and out of his line of sight, I couldn't resist. I unplugged the sign and grabbed it off the wall. I'd never finished a beer sign hunt empty handed and I wasn't about to that day.

As I was showing Bruce and Whit the sign outside, a large hand gripped my shoulder from behind. The bartender in his rusty butcher's apron had apparently followed me out. He said, "I'll fix your little wagon," then steered me back inside and made me hang the sign up while he went to call the police. That gave me the opening I needed and out the door I scooted, down the street and around the corner — the three of us running for our lives before catching a bus back to peaceful, sleepy Watertown. My little wagon did not get fixed that day, but my beer sign hunting days were officially over.

There apparently was a history of bad blood between "townies" and Taft students, just as the Student Handbook stated in its one-line warning against students hanging out at the fence in front of the school. Had I lived on the other side of that fence, I'd have resented "Tafties," too, especially if they sat out on the rails and attracted the attention of local girls who might be looking for more promising male attention.

I'd picked up Cream's first album, *Fresh Cream*, at Watertown's only music store and it blew a lot of minds when I played it in the lower mid common room. It had come out before I left Los Angeles, so I was familiar with the songs. The opening track, "I Feel Free," struck a powerful double chord with Bruce, Whit, Peter Byerly and others hearing it for the first time. The song's expression of joy about feeling free made us painfully aware of how little freedom we had at Taft. After playing it over and over, the least we could do was attire ourselves in bell-bottom jeans and paisley psychedelic shirts in allegiance to our heroes.

Miraculously a clothing store in Watertown had bell bottoms and paisley shirts. I decided to wear mine back to Taft while Bruce and Peter chose to carry theirs. Walking up the main street with its hooded yellow traffic signals, we decided to take a shortcut. We were halfway through our cut across a small parking lot when some townies appeared out of nowhere and surrounded us. Their leader was a boy about my age and size. He told me to take off my pants. It seemed like an odd request and an impossible ask. But as I looked around at their group, which included several girls, I could see he was serious. I told him no and then he closed the gap between us and made a second request, inches from my face. Again, I told him no and he threw the first punch.

It was a very short fight. One of the girls shouted "no" or "stop it" and that was it. They left almost as quickly as they'd appeared. All I remember is throwing one punch that landed squarely on someone's nose and feeling a satisfying juicy squish. Bruce and Peter had not gotten involved. I felt invigorated for having stood my ground and at the same time disappointed in them for not jumping in. I may have had a bloody nose and a few bruises but

I was otherwise unhurt. The girl who cried "stop" probably saved me from a thorough beating. By the time we got back to Taft, I was so full of adrenalin that I ditched Bruce and Peter and went to Jon Turak's room to see if he wanted to help me gather a posse of our toughest lower mids and go back to Watertown. I was amped up and eager to fight. But in my bell bottoms I probably looked more like the fey boy on a box of Crackerjacks than a street fighting man. Jon politely declined my invitation to get him into trouble.

My polka-dot bikini girl in *Surfer* magazine did her best to cheer me up but I was starting to worry and resent the power she had over me. I missed the sweaty, frenzied dances at Revere Teens and at the Palisades YMCA. I missed the parties at Raoul's house where we played spin the bottle and truth or dare with girls who seemed to enjoy those heart-pounding games as much as we did. I felt stuck in a time machine, surrounded by males, with nothing but a tiny picture of a girl in a bikini to remind me of one of the things I missed most about California. Late at night, after pleasuring myself carefully so Chip wouldn't hear, I would drift off to sleep. Sometimes I wondered if, just as my body was changing, perhaps my mind would change too. Was there something ahead in my development I didn't know was coming? Was I sent to Taft so some metamorphosis could take place without embarrassing my parents or me? Was I supposed to explore or slide into a relationship with another boy — like Phineas and Gene Forrester in *A Separate Peace*? We happened to be reading that book in Mr. Kusterer's class. Was that just a coincidence, or to prepare us? Did my parents know something I didn't? Taft seemed a ripe environment for all that. And Mr. Marx, with his toga hop parties and sexual banter, had already made it clear that being a prude was no way to act at Taft. If all that was true, I wanted no part of it. But then again, I knew I had no obvious control or rational understanding as to why I was attracted to girls in the first place. I just was. For the time being, anyway.

When my struggles with lower mid Latin became known, Mr. Marx made an offer he wouldn't let me refuse. He insisted we get up early, long before the rising bell, when it was still dark out. He'd lead me upstairs to the common room to tutor me. In his pajamas. After several weeks, he finally gave up, declaring me a lost cause when it came to Latin before once more offering me his standard line of mildly encouraging discouragement: I was probably better suited for other things at Taft.

CHAPTER 11

As badly as I wanted out of Taft, flunking or getting kicked out were not options. For one thing, I no longer wanted to live at home. I didn't understand my parents and they didn't understand me. I also didn't know what I wanted to do later in life, but the value of a good education had been drilled so deeply into me that I was afraid if I didn't do well in school, statistically speaking I probably would end up a failure. According to my parents' latest revision on the importance of getting good grades, all my grades prior to Taft miraculously no longer mattered. Colleges would accept (or reject) me based solely on my performance at Taft. I was starting to believe if the things I was witnessing at Taft were a harbinger of college, count me out. Until then, I was determined not to flunk out. If and when I left, it would be on my terms — not theirs.

More than anything else, rock and roll gave me hope for a better future and a coping mechanism for the present. Songs like "Fortunate Son," took direct aim at Vietnam and the institutions and old boy networks that supported it. Taft was the perfect environment to supercharge music from the sixties that offered visions of better, alternative lifestyles for my generation. While boarding schools were too exclusive and isolated to be a popular target for protest songs, they were proving, at least to me, to be one of the better examples of tyranny if you happened to be trapped inside one. Inspired by rock music, I was determined to not let Taft dictate my future or alter my values. When I came to the realization that I was stuck in the belly of a beast with no easy way out, a seed took hold. I started thinking about how I could take down what was trying to destroy me without destroying myself.

I forgave Bruce for standing down in the fight with the townies. I doubt he even registered I was mad at him. We were fairly open and honest with each other, so while I might have said something, the air cleared pretty quickly. We resumed our late-night bull sessions in the stairwells and for a brief while life returned to normal. That is, in between the dull surprises that were never in short supply.

One Saturday evening I saw a group of lower mids crowded around the senior monitor desk on my way to Bruce's room. They called me over. Normally I detoured around the senior mon on duty, but this was Cam Clark's night at the helm and he was one of the more rakish seniors and Taft's best-known tray dropper. Listen to the Carly Simon song "You're So Vain" and you've got an accurate description of Taft's star soccer goalie and all-around senior stud. Dropping my guard, I went over to see what the commotion was about.

On the table lay Cam's Nikon camera, along with several glossy black and white photographs, all developed in high resolution, all of the same object from different points of view, but otherwise a mystery to me — like another Rorschach test. I was ready to walk when one of the boys asked me what I thought I was looking at. I shrugged, not really interested in photographs in general and arty ones in particular, but their chides went up a notch and I took the bait. I studied one and then another as closely as I could until I was sure I'd figured it out. "The Mississippi Delta," I replied. I could almost picture Cam taking the shot from his father's U2 spy plane with a WASPy debutant perched on his lap. Cam leaned back in his chair, enjoying yet another lower mid suckered into mistaking a close -up shot of female genitalia for something else. As he explained it, there was a studio in New York City where Tafties could photograph "models" for a very reasonable price. I'd taken a bus or train into NYC one Sunday earlier in the year and bought some records at Sam Goody's followed by a hot dog at a Zum Zum restaurant. I don't remember how I got there or how I got back, but there were obviously places in New York I'd missed that welcomed preppies with open arms and more. That night, I studied the picture of my polka dot bikini girl in a new and worried light.

I think it was sometime between Thanksgiving and Christmas break when Chip told me he'd found another roommate. With Frank Kelly gone, there was at least one extra bed on the fourth floor. I seconded the idea. It would give me more privacy at night and end the cold war between us. The only downside was that I would have to deal with Mr. Marx's intrusions alone. By then I thought I knew him well enough that I could handle them and that they couldn't get any worse than what I was already used to.

As the days grew shorter, the mood at Taft turned grim. There was often nothing better to do than hunker down in my room and crank open the radiator valve. Windowpanes were starting to condense, the lawns had turned brown and hard, and the trees without their leaves looked dead. By the time football practice was over, the sun had long since set and there was very little natural light when I got back to my room. Under the circumstances, there was nothing much else to do except to study, which the masters seemed to factor in. Their homework assignments increased in proportion to the bleak days of rain, sleet and eventually snow.

Mr. Marx's visits to my room did not let up after Chip was gone. After athletics and before vespers, and then again after study hall and before lights out. It did not matter if I was studying for a test or trying to complete a homework assignment. If he wanted to come in, there was nothing I could do. He never talked about the news, current events or himself. It was almost always about me and how I was doing — followed by how he thought I was doing. He would tell me that I needed to accept that I was on the East Coast for good and to forget California because I was never going back. He would say this, sometimes with a hint of sympathy, but more often he would mock or tease me about it to snap me out of my funk. He was the only master at Taft who showed any interest in me on a personal level, so I assumed that all masters at Taft regarded me the same way he did — only he had the honesty to say the things he did to my face.

On his way out of my room he would tell me I might eventually learn how to "fit in" at Taft. His visits were mentally exhausting but never dull because I never knew which version of Mr. Marx was going to show up. I had even less desire to fit into Taft than when I had none to begin with, but there was no reason to tell him that. He knew what I thought about Taft. And all he had *was* Taft. It wasn't a case of opposites attracting, but more like an electron and proton bound together by a nucleus. When he went back across the hall to his apartment and I was left alone with my thoughts, I often found myself wondering more about him than me. I knew I didn't fit in, but in some ways, he was almost as much an outsider as I was. He was so unlike any adult I'd ever been around that sometimes I couldn't help feeling a pang of sympathy toward him.

Not long after Chip left, something woke me in the middle of the night. Although it was pitch black, I could see the outline of a person standing in my doorway. I assumed it was Mr. Marx but as my eyes adjusted, I realized it was someone else. The person did not move or say a word but just kept watching me in silence until I eventually made out who he was.

"Mr. Jacobs," I said, trying not to sound too alarmed, "What are you doing here?"

Mr. Jacobs didn't reply and so I asked him again. This time he answered in a high stuttering whisper — apologizing that he was returning the broom that I had left in the stairwell during work program earlier the same day. I thanked him and to my relief his silhouette melted away. Puzzled by what had just happened, I looked at my clock and saw it was late, very late — somewhere between two and three in the morning. Mr. Jacobs was not one of my teachers. And though I did not know where his apartment was, I knew it was nowhere near my room and most likely in another part of the school since I'd never seen him on the HTD wing before. There was no reason for him to return my broom in the middle of the night. Why would he do that? The more I thought about it, the more unsettled I became. I already knew Mr. Marx was strange. But this proved he wasn't the only one. Most of the masters at Taft were single and it got me to wondering. How many more were like them?

Mr. Jacobs

Many of them had nicknames that you could solve only by asking upperclassmen how they got them. There was "Beezer", the flamboyantly attired Spanish master who took boys for rides on weekends in his prized convertible. Mr. Greene was "Thumper." Mr. Curry was "Fog" or "Foggy." Others included "Plumber Dick," "Fairy John," "Nasty Al," "Deputy Dog," "Tojo Rick," and "Booger Bob." Mr. Jacobs was referred to as "Jake the Snake" for reasons unknown to me, but it seemed appropriate.

Leonard Sargent was just "Sarge." Sarge reportedly owned a cattle ranch in Montana, where he would invite a select group of Taft students on "a working vacation" each summer. He was married, but if his wife came out to visit him, it was once in a blue moon. I think I remember seeing her once because, if I recall correctly, she did have the rather handsome, weathered face of an outdoorsy woman. What kind of man leaves a wife in charge of his ranch to teach nine months a year at an all-boys prep school two thousand miles away? A highly dedicated one, I suppose. As long as the masters at Taft didn't try to pry into my personal life, I had no business or interest peering into theirs.

Mr. Jacobs never approached me again but he opened my eyes to something I hadn't paid much attention to before. Few, if any masters, had female visitors. It was unusual to see a woman or girl not associated with the school, walking down the main corridor. When one did, it was not unusual to see a master look down and grimace while the rest of us tried to keep our eyeballs from popping out. Seniors would invite their girlfriends over from St. Margaret's or Westover to watch a home game on Saturday afternoons, but other than that, most female visitors to Taft must have felt as comfortable as the frogs in Mr. Reiff's biology class.

The exception to that was when girls were bused in for a Taft "mixer." Those poor girls. Wearing their finest dresses and long white gloves, herded onto yellow school buses, transported to Taft, offloaded, lined up, and marched single file along one end of the Taft Library to meet their fates. We lined up on the other end, pasting down our cowlicks with spit, brushing the dandruff off our sports coats, squeezing zits and blotting the sweat off our foreheads with our white pocket handkerchiefs. Taft chaperones, including Mr. Marx, lined up like wolves on one side next to tables covered with cookie platters and crystal punch bowls, while female chaperones lined up like nervous lambs along the opposite wall. There was a call for hush and when the nervous chatter died down, a needle was set on a scratchy record and a solemn promenade came out of the speakers. The first couple in each line met at the fifty-yard line and an arm was extended followed by a white glove that received it, and the festivities were formally underway.

With a hundred or so such pairings it took a while. Boys and girls of the same minority race were strategically placed in line so that they always paired off with each other. From our side of the picket line, a cheer would go up from time to time when a girl took the arm of her date. The girl in the spotlight would smile and blush as she was led to the punch bowl by her knight in shining armor, oblivious to the fact that her unattractiveness had just put her escort in the running for winning the ugly duckling bet. Foxtrots, dogtrots and every other kind of trot followed, all under the gaze of chaperones ready to step in if the rules regarding spatial distancing started to break down, such as a hand slipping below the lower back, or pelvises that weren't following Taft's laws of magnetic repulsion. The dances always ended in a draw. But with the scent of sweet perfume lingering on our clothes long after the girls were bused back to the safety of their school, the lonesome bed springs at Taft tallied the toll those mixers took.

When Christmas break arrived, I looked forward to going home about as much as I did a Taft mixer. Greenwich was grey and cold. The lawn where I'd spent so many hours honing my wide receiver skills had quit photosynthesizing. It had turned to brown tundra or mush depending on which side of 32 the outdoor thermometer read. The only two warm places in the house were the kitchen and the den where my father stoked the fireplace

Family photo with my father's parents, Christmas 1968 in Greenwich, Connecticut

morning, noon and night. I'd prop myself up on some pillows on the floor and watch a football game or reruns of *Gilligan's Island*, wishing I was stranded on a desert island with Mary Ann and Ginger. My father would do paperwork at his desk in the same room but we did not talk much. My mother spent most of her time in the kitchen, heating up a saucepan with some kind of sulfur salt. She dipped a dish towel into it and let it cool before applying it to her face, which had developed a rash.

I developed a rash of my own. A severe case of jock itch that I discovered by accident while soaking in the tub one evening. I subconsciously scratched while I was reading a book, and that ignited a firestorm. For the next three hours I took the bathroom scrub brush to it every five minutes until it was raw and bleeding, and still the urge to scratch returned, each time worse than before. If I'd had a steel-wire brush, I'd be walking around today with two seeds and no pod.

At 14 I was too old for toys but unfortunately the right age for things like sweaters, Pendleton shirts, ties and sport coats. Every article of clothing I got was a subtle nudge to look the part of a "nice young man" smartly turned out to make a good reflection on the parents. Appearances were far more important to them than I was. Every article of clothing I received was like a little emotional shiv. I wanted Christmas to be happy and I wanted to make my parents happy. But they were trying to mold me into someone I wasn't.

The only "fun" present my mother gave me was a Snurfer, a primitive snowboard. It was shaped like a short, wide water ski with a rope attached to the nose. It had snowed recently and I ventured out one afternoon to try it in our back yard. I walked up the short, steep slope with several ornamental rocks poking through. With my mother looking on hopefully through the kitchen window, I made several attempts. Unable to steer it, I wound up crashing into the rocks. I felt depressed for being such a failure. When I saw how sad my mother looked, I suddenly started feeling much better. It took a few more spills to figure out why. And then it came to me: my failing in front of her was the perfect way to get back at her for *making* me a failure. Merry Christmas, Mom and Dad — you've raised a cropper.

Me, Christmas 1968, Greenwich, Connecticut

The problems between my mother and father remained a secret that they would not confide to me until years later. Had I known about their issues at the time, I might have seen them in a different light — as two people struggling just like I was. As it was, our house remained cold and divided, literally and figuratively. The monstrosity they were building on Quail Road was on the street where the Barnards lived. Biff Barnard was a graduate of Taft and Mr. Cunningham's assistant director of admissions. Biff sought me out sometime during my lower mid year, telling me what a happy coincidence it was that we were going to be neighbors. Happy coincidence my ass. Over Christmas my parents took me to the construction site and, as proud and thrilled as they were walking around the huge foundation up to their ankles in freezing mud, I was moved in another direction. I would rather live in a cave.

CHAPTER 12

My parents lived in San Jose after they married in 1944. When the war ended, my father was still enlisted and was transferred to Washington, D.C. They lived there for about a year until he was discharged and moved to Middlebury to start their family. My father put aside his pre-war plan of becoming a surgeon and went to work for his father at Anaconda. They had a ready-made social life as most of my father's childhood friends still lived in Middlebury. Being from California, my mother had a harder time fitting in at first. We belonged to the Highfield Country Club and Cliffside on Lake Quassapaug. My parents threw many cocktail parties at our home on Breakneck Hill. I can still recall the tinkling of ice and the rattle of bracelets as their friends would come into my room, highballs in hand, to steal a glimpse into my crib where I would listen to their oohs and aahs, wondering what the fuss was all about.

Los Angeles was a harder fit for them socially. Early on, a neighbor across the street, Mrs. Frye, invited my mother over for a mid-morning visit. My mother showed up on time to find the front door slightly ajar. After several knocks on the door, it opened wider and my mother called out "hello." There came a strange sounding hello back. Not one to pre-judge someone's voice, my mother exchanged several hellos back and forth with what turned out to be the Frye's mynah bird. Mrs. Frye, morning drink in hand, eventually showed up.

By the time we moved to Greenwich, my parents were skilled at making new friends, and they would trot me out whenever someone stopped by. I would hear the doorbell ring, the familiar sound of fake happy voices, followed by my father's dreaded foot-steps up the stairs and the knock on my door. Afterward, there would be a critique about my posture and less than enthusiastic showing. A poor showing on my part would lead into another family ritual I was getting used to: "Constructive criticism" at dinnertime.

"Mr. Marx writes that you're still having trouble fitting in." That seemed to concern them the most about me. I respected my parents. I knew they had been through many more challenges than I had. I knew they cared about me. So how could they be so clueless? Unless they weren't. I already hated my parents for sending me to Taft and hated them more for not taking me out when I asked. I saw no point in making matters worse and so I kept my feelings to myself. I did not want to give them another opportunity for me to hate them more than I already did. The damage was done and the disconnect nearly complete.

My parents drove me back to begin winter term. There was the pep talk to do better. My father called me "Bright Eyes" and told me to cheer up, smile and "buckle down," that everything would turn out all right.

I'd always watched the nightly news with my parents. Now it was just the occasional glimpse of the war, and only if Mr. Marx left his door open with the TV on. The Vietnam war was an occasional topic at vespers. Guest speakers, invited to make arguments both for and against the war, were usually introduced by Mr. Esty with a short biography touting their credentials. Both sides of the war were covered — from why it was necessary to prevent communism, to why it was wrong on philosophical, class, racial and moral grounds. In general, students at Taft opposed the war and there would be stomps and cheers when a liberal guest speaker of a Daniel Berrigan type argued against it. But we also heard from pro-war speakers, which satisfied the student minority with ROTC aspirations who cheered in rebuttal. Whatever the speaker and whatever the subject, Mr. Esty relished introducing illustrious speakers to enlighten us. Never mind the paralyzing effect most of these speeches had on students like me. They seemed designed to provide a forum for genteel scholarly debate on both sides of an issue from a nice, safe distance. "What's that you say, Mrs. Robinson? Joltin' Joe has left and gone away."

The winter term marked the seniors' last chance to raise their grades. Some already had the grades they needed and had applied for early admissions while others were on the cusp or had taken one too many "gut" classes and now had to complete the harder courses they'd avoided. For the rest of us, the bitter cold New England weather forced us to remain in our rooms. The masters piled on the work to help keep us occupied.

Hockey was to Taft what the Packers are to Green Bay. The head varsity coach was Mr. Sargent. His assistant coach was Mr. Odden — Mr. Esty's chosen successor who would eventually replace him as Taft's headmaster. The varsity team was led that year by a mid prodigy from Duluth, Rick Heimbach. The hockey team (along with Mr. Stone's football team) recruited ringers to compete against rival schools that did the same. The passion for hockey was evident from the beginning when games would break out on the fourth-floor corridor on Saturday and Sunday nights. Most of the students at Taft were from New England and grew up playing hockey, so there was plenty of home-grown talent.

Hotchkiss, Choate, Loomis and several other schools along with Taft were in the Housatonic League. For whatever reason, Hotchkiss was our main sporting rival. Our hockey game with them that year was at Hotchkiss and attendance by the student body was close to mandatory. Several buses lined up one bright cold morning. We climbed aboard for the hour or so drive. As I recall there was a roof over the rink that extended above the wooden stands but the back was open to the elements. We arrived at the end of the junior varsity match. By the time the varsity game started, the temperature had dipped into the teens and my teeth were chattering. I was more concerned about how I was going to stay warm than I was with Mr. Marx sidling up next to me in the stands and handing me a Coke. It was a nice gesture and though I would have preferred a hot chocolate, down the hatch it went.

Before long, as I walked down through the stands and made my way to the restroom, I became aware that Mr. Marx was following me. There was a row of un-partitioned urinals against the wall. I walked up to one, unzipped and was about to do my business

when Mr. Marx came up to the stall next to mine. I tried to go
but with him looking down at me, my bladder would not release.
I gave up and headed back to the stands.

This pattern repeated itself two or three more times. Each time
my need to relieve myself became more urgent than the last, but
he followed me in each time and stood next to me, not saying
a word, just leering down at me. It became a game within the
game, and I was losing. Shut out in fact. I could not go with
him standing there. I spent the last period of the game willing
the clock to wind down. During the bus ride back to Taft, my
eyes were watering and I was afraid my bladder would burst. I
still find it difficult to relieve myself in a public restroom with
anyone standing next to me unless I'm pretty hammered. One
of the many legacies Taft has passed on to me.

For my winter sport I chose basketball and made the lower school
team. What I lacked in height, quickness and skill I made up
for in enthusiasm. I loved basketball. My friends and I loved the
Lakers and John Wooden's UCLA Bruins were a dynasty. The
problem with the Bruins was they won so often their games were
hardly a contest and frankly boring. The Lakers, on the other
hand, were very good but they still played second fiddle to the
Celtics. We all played basketball at the park and year-round in
neighborhood driveways, with fantasies of playing for the Lakers
and beating the Celtics.

We modeled our games after the stars. We would practice their
signature moves over and over until we mastered them — or
thought we had. From Dave Bing's corkscrew, Dick Barnett's
bank shot, Lew Alcindor's skyhook to Wilt the Stilt's finger roll.

Shooting a two-handed set shot would earn you the same look as if you were dancing the Charleston. I spent hours practicing jump shots — building my strength and learning how to release the ball when I reached the apex. Along with Jerry West, the other Laker star, Elgin Baylor, had a magical double-clutch move under the basket, where he'd pump his knees after he was airborne and somehow remain aloft, long after his defender fell helplessly back to earth.

Taft had two indoor gyms. One was modern with pullout bleachers and a new electronic scoreboard. That's where the varsity and JV teams played. The other was the old gym, where pickup games on the weekends were open to all-comers and where the lower school team played.

Our lower school coach was the bowtie-wearing Mr. Gould. I had already played in one or two pick-up games on Sundays, including one with a good, tough, one-armed player named John Lisakolsky. Despite hockey's stature at Taft, there was a lot of interest in basketball and as the Sunday games proved, there were a lot of good players. My hopes for the same experience on the lower school team started high, but quickly curdled.

About my grandfather's age, Mr. Gould took an approach to basketball that dated to Dr. Naismith's invention of the game. I got the feeling he wanted to take down the rims and nets and replace them with peach baskets. Showboating of any kind was met with a persnickety frown. He quickly set about imposing his vision of the game. Our practices were twenty minutes of dribbling exercises followed by twenty minutes of wind sprints followed by twenty minutes of two-handed ball passing.

Every movement on the court was examined in detail, and bad habits like behind-the-back passes and double clutching were frowned upon.

One of Mr. Gould's favorite drills was the figure eight. Three players would start at one end, and without dribbling the ball, weave in and out down the court, completing pass after pass until finishing with a layup at the other end — all without any defenders trying to stop them. No defenders were necessary as the ball rarely remained in bounds past half-court. About a month or so into this and before our first regular league game, we boarded a bus to scrimmage against an all-black inner-city school in Hartford. Their free-flowing play was no match for our highly disciplined, intelligent approach. They ran circles around us and we were thoroughly trounced.

On club basketball team, Winter 1968-69. I'm in the back row, second from the left. My growth spurt hadn't yet kicked in.

This time I wasn't going to let a coach take the joy out of another sport I loved. Taft had a club system, where every new student was arbitrarily assigned to be either an alpha, gamma or beta throughout their career. If you chose not to play on a road team, you had to play an intramural sport for whatever club you belonged to. I quit the lower school squad and joined the "A" league Gamma team — a mix of seniors and upper mids — some in it for a lark and others who were good athletes staying in shape for their spring varsity sport. It was relaxed, and I could double clutch without fear of being benched. It proved to be a good pivot away from my first two coaches at Taft, whose ultra-studious approaches were taking the fun out of playing what, after all, is just a game.

There was one big plus with Chip gone. I did not have to hide my relationship with the pink polka dot bikini girl in my *Surfer* magazine anymore. I could freely gaze at her after basketball and before lights out without feeling self-conscious or spied upon. What was she doing while I was cooped up in an all-boys school? It pained me to think. She was probably hanging out with a buff surfer in Hawaii with a plumeria flower in her hair while he rubbed tanning oil all over her. Was her life as perfect as it looked, or was something missing? If she only knew how perfect I thought she was. Would that count for anything? And if she could only look inside my soul and see what I was going through, would that be enough to sway her to consider a pasty wretch like me? I knew she had the power to save me. She was also torture and tantalizingly out of reach. Part of me knew she was an unhealthy fantasy but given my reality at Taft, I came to accept her presence in my life for the salvation she gave me and the peaceful night's sleep that followed.

As Mr. Marx's uninvited visits to my room continued, he focused more on personal matters. How I was doing in school didn't seem to concern him anymore. That was a matter of record and we both knew I was an average student by Taft standards. It was as though my letting him down academically entitled him to take breaks from preparing his next day's lessons for the high achievers and let off some steam by visiting me. When I'd ignore him, he would try to tickle me to lighten me up. If he went too far and wouldn't stop, I'd be forced to fight back and then we would have a brief wrestling match that would end when Mr. Marx finally gave up. Sometimes when he left my room, I got the impression he liked me and would report good things to my parents. Other times, he would leave in a huff, dismissing me as a prude, dipshit, virgin or teaser.

The communal bathroom at the end of the hall was ostensibly for Willie and me. It did not have a radiator for heat, so in the winter the bathroom mirror would fog up. I was showering one evening and saw a hand wipe away the condensation. I looked through the curtain and saw Mr. Marx mouth the word "nudie," in the mirror as he looked at me. It was another one of his pet names for me. There was nothing I could do about it. As long as he didn't get violent again, and I could make my escapes late at night and smoke in the stairwell with Bruce and friends, I thought I could survive him until June.

PART 4

Looking Through a Glass Onion

"Your ass is grass." That was the first thing Woody Chase said to me when I cut in front of him in the dinner line to chat with Bruce. Woody was Bruce's French teacher, taking over for Bruce's regular teacher the same way Gross and Reed had taken over for Mr. Oscarson. Bruce had told me Woody was cool, and I could see that while my butting in line irritated him, he was going to let it pass because I was Bruce's friend. Most seniors would have given me a shove and told me to get back in line. Woody was of medium build with a round, pleasant face.

"He's cool," Bruce told Woody, referring to me. Coming from California, I thought that was a given. And the sooner I could slip that fact in, the sooner this Woody character would stop looking down at me so completely unimpressed. And with that the dining room doors opened and we herded in to find what culinary mysteries awaited.

At our next stairwell smoke, Bruce had some good news. Woody had a room in the ISP wing of the school — Independent Studies Project — where seniors who been "accepted for special projects" lived. The major perk of living in the ISP wing was that it was basically off limits to masters. In return for this trust, ISP students were expected to adhere to the rules without supervision. If we could make it to ISP wing after lights out, Woody told Bruce, we could hang out. From a cold stairwell to a penthouse? I was on board.

The risk of getting caught was far greater but so was the reward. We finished our butts while timing our next outing around a monitor-less night and figuring out what route we would take. We set out a few nights later, later than usual to reduce our chances of getting caught. I met Bruce at the juncture of the fourth-floor landing where Mr. Sargent lived. We waited several minutes, listening for any masters or mons who might be roaming the floors below. Satisfied that the coast was clear, we started down with all the stealth, fear and thrill of a prison break, knowing if we were caught below the fourth floor, we would have no plausible excuse for being there. And our "asses" would indeed be "grass."

Reaching the first floor we peered around the main corridor with its red terra cotta tile. A dimly illuminated no-man's land. We were amazed we had made it that far but we still had a long way to go. Bruce carried his brown hard-sole shoes. I wore my blue sneakers. The main hall was eerie still. Mr. Esty's office was directly across from us. No light on. There rarely was. We turned right, down the few steps into the dining hall anteroom, and crossed over to our next and last leg, the hallway that paralleled the dining hall that led directly to the ISP wing.

We held our breath as one of us turned the handle on the wooden door, like we were pulling the pin on a grenade. We opened the door a crack and peered down the long hallway. No one there. There was another closed door at the opposite end. Every door, every hallway, every corner we came to reminded me of the TV show *Let's Make a Deal*. Where a goat was yours if you picked the wrong door, or a brand-new convertible if you picked the right one. Our nerves were frayed. We were nearly there. All we had to do was get past this one last door. I was sure Oscie or Rudy Schaffer, the mon who'd once confiscated my transistor radio, was waiting on the side, ready to fix our little wagons, as the bartender in Waterbury had once threatened me, the minute we opened it. Our little wagons probably did need fixing, or at least a tune-up, for all the rules we were breaking. Bruce turned the handle anyway, and the door opened. The coast was clear. Our little wagons were good to go.

The ground floor had the musty smell of an old hotel lobby, with dark wood paneling, dingy carpeting and little candelabra sconces that flickered like old whale-oil lamps. There was a large room off to the right with a round poker table in the center, an old chandelier above it and a few dilapidated couches and easy chairs with the stuffing coming out of them. As we tiptoed up a creaky flight of stairs to get to the second or third floor, we began hearing laughter and music from some of the rooms we passed. There may have been name placards on the doors. I think that was how we found the room we were looking for. When Woody opened the door, there was a haze of incense and cigarette smoke and the stereo was cranking out music I'd never heard before. What I was hearing for the first time was *Music from Big Pink*, The Band's first album. We were ushered in, and a whole new world was about to open up. A place where the inmates were in control of the asylum.

Taped above Woody's bed was a centerfold with watermel-on-shaped breasts dangling down at me. Sim Johnson, Woody's roommate, lay on his bed, reading the *Playboy* interview with a look of sharp irritation. In short order, Sim began to refer to Bruce and me as "the kindergarten." His disgust eventually got so bad that a month later he moved out. And George Fleeson, a Kansas boy who read *Playboy* for the pictures, took his place.

I wondered why Woody would invite a couple of lower mids to his room. Seniors were gods. We were so far down the totem pole that we were practically invisible. The only housewarming gifts we showed up with were gratitude and Bruce's cigarettes. I think we caught Woody off guard. Maybe he saw in us a reflection of himself when he was our age. Or maybe he saw us as a couple of refugees on the run. Either way, he let us in and didn't seem to give it a second thought. He didn't care what Sim or any of the other ISP seniors thought, even though our being there put them all at risk. All he seemed to care about, and ask in return, was our willingness to listen and learn at the feet of "Teach" — Woody's *nom de plume* at Taft.

Woody's father was a foreign diplomat somewhere in the Middle East. I gathered they were close and Woody had spent a lot of time there. He had strong pro-Arab sentiments, but the Vietnam War was such a much bigger deal at the time that almost no one at Taft seemed to care. I think that bothered Woody and led to this: If his views about the Middle East were going to be marginalized at Taft, he would teach the marginalized in return. Bruce and I were the first of several lower mids living on the margins of curiosity who would eventually seek him out.

Fortunately, there were plenty of other topics besides the Middle East that came up in late-night bull sessions. They drew in other seniors from all over ISP. They would stop by for a cigarette and end up staying for an hour or two before going back to their rooms. The conversations were great. We hung on every word. Every now and again there would be a knock on the door, a warning that the lone master who resided there, Mr. Logan, was out wandering the halls. Bruce and I would scurry to the back of Woody's closet and remove a set of un-grouted bricks that we would crawl through. On the other side was a sparsely furnished room, tall enough to stand in and large enough for a pool table. It looked like a construction error or maybe the architect had a soft spot for bootleggers. Either way, it was about as good a hideaway as we could ask for. The "cave" behind the back of the closet only deepened the air of intrigue at Woody's salon.

Woody wasn't a joiner and definitely not a follower. The BFD movement? Way too parochial. Taft was already in his rear-view mirror. I believe he had early acceptance to Harvard in hand. He was not into sports, but had a broad range of other interests — from music to movies, to poetry and literature. Woody gave off the impression he had a girl in every port, but boasting about it would be *de-class-say*. And when all these things about him came through to me over time, California suddenly seemed provincial by comparison.

Bruce and I absorbed all we could. He was teaching us so much about life that our parents' tuition checks should have been going to him. Woody could separate the ridiculous from the sublime when it came to the *avant-garde*. Nothing ruffled him. You could disappoint him, but I never saw him stoop to anger. The only thing he looked down on was anything or anyone that struck him as *bourgeois* — which I vaguely took to mean people with stolid middle and upper middle-class values — people like my parents, grandparents — and potentially me.

Woody saw himself as mentor to lower mids who were willing to listen and learn all these things from him. Bruce and I were definitely in that camp. But while others visited his room during daylight hours and thumbed through the *Playboy* magazines

Woody Chase (back row, second from left, in sweater), and his roommate, George Fleeson (front row, second from left, with cigar), and grateful lower mids.

scattered around like mousetraps, we were more interested in the late-night escapes and the roadhouse atmosphere. From Quicksilver Messenger Service's *Happy Trails*, the Beatles' "White Album," Bob Dylan's *Blonde on Blonde*, Miles Davis, Aretha Franklin — there was almost always a record playing. But the one I would have crawled through mud and under barbed wire to listen to was The Band's *Music from Big Pink*.

In Los Angeles, where the Beach Boys were still outpolling the Beatles in popularity contests on AM radio stations before I left, there was nothing like The Band. As I studied them (and their next of kin) in the photograph inside the album cover, I was struck how they not only dressed like my childhood heroes Davy Crockett and Daniel Boone, but in my mind, they *sounded* like those guys would have if they were still alive and formed a band. My exile at Taft was the reason their music meant so much to me. Richard Manuel's opening track, "We Can Talk," offered me hope that my parents and I could one day talk openly with each other as equals. "Chest Fever," with its opening ethereal organ that dives into a swampy blues-rock crawl, was a reality check that I might be in over my head when it came to my polka dot bikini girl — or any girl for that matter. And lyrically my favorite, "Caledonia Mission," about an attempt to rescue a lover from a convent, kept my most pathetic dream alive: That someone out there would rescue me from Taft and take me to "a place they'll never find." My bikini girl photo notwithstanding, I had no expectations that such a girl existed in the flesh. No expectations at all.

On average, we probably made the trek to ISP once a week that winter. It was a harrowing journey and if the risks of getting

caught were greater, it only made the rewards sweeter. If we were
caught, we would be put on bounds, grounded on weekends. Mr.
Oscarson would decide the punishment and Mr. Marx would be
informed and perhaps institute late-night bed checks.

One night, on our way back from Woody's, we heard voices in
the dining hall anteroom. We were forced to make our way back
down the corridor to the safety zone of ISP and wait. Every ten
or fifteen minutes we would try again, only to hear the same
voices. It was getting on toward 2 a.m., and we would need a few
hours of sleep if we were going to function. Out of options, we
decided to bypass the lobby and go outdoors. I was dressed for
Los Angeles. It was a clear, moonlit night and frost was hatching
on the window panes.

There had been a big winter storm a day or two before. During
the day, it had warmed up enough so the snow on the surface
started to melt. Now the temperature had plunged, and in a tee
shirt, jeans and tennis shoes I was rudely introduced to the laws
of thermodynamics. The outdoor path we were on was a sheet
of black ice. The first door we came to was locked, so we set
off again, this time off the path and on top of the snow, which
glittered like diamonds but turned out to be a nightmare to
walk on. The crust on top was glazed over with solid ice half an
inch thick. At our weight we did not break through. Without
purchase, we slipped and slid our way on top of the crust until
we reached another door that was fortunately unlocked.

We met in the stairwell the next evening after lights out and told
the tale of how close we'd come to freezing to death. With the
moon streaming into the stairwell and the temperature outside

still well below freezing, an idea grabbed hold of us so sponta-
neously that we ran back to our rooms, put on every stitch of
warm clothing we had, and headed down to the kitchen with its
stacks of aluminum trays.

Above the baseball field was a recently plowed service road.
Rising above that was the snow-covered golf course that Taft
shared with Watertown. We threw our trays over the snowbank,
clambered up over icy broken chunks of snow and looked up at
the hills of pristine silvery whiteness illuminated by a moon that
was almost too bright to look at.

We made our way to a line of pines where the snow was clumpier
from slough off the limbs. We followed each other's shadows
uphill. When we came to the end of the stand, we made our way
across a flat to another line of trees going up, and then another
until we were halfway up, looking down at sleepy Taft in the
distance. Huffing and puffing, our lungs burning from the cold,
we sat down on our trays.

I had my doubts about what lay ahead. I'd broken my collarbone
in a toboggan crash at the bottom of Hetzel's hill when I was a
child and that was in full daylight. When there's no way to steer
or brake, you either have faith or you don't. We crossed our
legs, lifted our gloves off the ice and gave ourselves up. Hoping
the same fates that had created such a crystal-clear night would
reward us for following their call.

I was hurtling straight toward the first line of trees as I reached
the bottom of the first hill. My eyes were streaming from the cold
air, making it hard to see or know when to bail when something

strange happened. The terrain leveled off and I began to decel-
erate. I slowed way down, like a lull on a roller coaster, and then
the terrain sloped down to the left and the tray began picking
up speed again. Bruce and Whit had caught up to me, and the
three of us were suddenly screaming toward the plowed road
and the high bank of snow dead ahead. We all bailed at the last
second, sliding the last ten feet into the snowbank as our trays
flew up and over. We sat there in silence for a bit and then started
laughing and couldn't stop. We'd finally found what we'd been
missing ever since our paper airplane days.

We took another run or two that night, minus the fear of the
unknown. As we walked back along the blacktop toward the
colorless buildings of Taft at night, we looked back up at the
snow-covered hills and saw that we had only scratched the surface.
The hills continued sloping up, well past our last starting point.

We knew we'd discovered something big and that we would do it
again the next night. Naturally we wanted to share our discovery.
Between classes the next day, we decided who to tell and who not
to. We came up with a short list but only two or three followed
us out the second night.

It was even better than the first. We had stomped enough holes
in the snowy crust and learned the quickest way up the hills the
first night, so we reached our original starting point in no time.
After one or two runs, we decided to climb higher. Three quarters
of the way to the top, we set off again. The run was twice as long
and just as good. High-speed slopes followed by glides across
flats to the top of the next hill, our trays followed the gentle
curves like they knew exactly where to go. All the way down to

the snowbank where we'd end up sprawled, splayed and covered with snow. Dusting off, we'd trek back up — happy, sweaty, and eager for more.

Word spread through class the next day and several lower mids approached us asking if they could join in. The third night we were ten or so strong and by the fourth night out we could have sold tickets. There were lines of students walking up to the very top for the quarter hour ride down. At some point, as Bruce, Whit and I were making another ascent and taking it all in, it dawned on us. We were witnessing the comatose awaken to the fact that childhood was short and there was fun to be had before they took it all away. In the same way we had with paper airplanes out Bruce's window in September, we were starting a second underground insurrection at Taft — and based on the number of students following us, we were back in business.

There was a short but very steep alternative run off the top that offered a different experience for those brave enough to try it. It ended at the far side of a pond — a water trap for duffers in summer, now solidly frozen over in winter and snowless. It was a short, dangerous ride. Once a rider reached the pond, not always a given, the tray seemed to accelerate as it streaked across to the bank on the far side. Riders would slam into the far bank like crash-test dummies, shake themselves off and climb up to do it again. John Hagelin, another lower mid with what would prove to be a psychotic attraction to high risk, liked this run in particular. When I'd get back to the top from one of my roller-coaster runs, I would watch him take this short death-defying ride while I caught my breath — watching as he bombed down the hill and shot across the pond, looking smaller and smaller until it seemed he would disappear altogether. Laying back on his tray like a luger, with his legs splayed out in front as he neared impact, his tray would hit the far bank with such force it would vault him high into the air and over the bank. A minute later he would reappear on top of the bank and wave — having stuck the landing on what looked like the far side of the moon.

Only one time he didn't. He hit the bank and fell back motionless. We all made our way down to see how bad it was. His tailbone had hit a water pipe that fed the pond. He was in a great deal of pain. Going to the Taft infirmary that time of night was out of the question. John somehow sucked it up and the next day he was walking again. John had a reputation as one of the smartest students in our class, but unlike Erik Kitchen and Bruce Braine, John's genius was in physics, astrophysics — and theories about space, time and dimensions that went way beyond anything most of us could begin to comprehend. He would go on to become one of the more enigmatic students in our class, ending up running for president of the United States in 1996 on the Natural Law ticket. The magic nights of sledding down Watertown's golf course on kitchen trays ended with his T-bone, but we had stuck a second spear into the Taft beast while it was sleeping — and Bruce and I felt good about that. We'd escaped, however briefly, the steady diet of classes, study hall, quizzes, tests and term papers — and had gotten others to follow.

CHAPTER 14

The demonstrations across colleges and universities were ramping up. There were sit-ins, protests and student takeovers of administration buildings. Tensions were ratcheting as groups like the Black Panthers, Students for a Democratic Society (SDS) and the Weather Underground were beginning to back up their demands for change with action "by any means necessary." Others like Ken Kesey, Neil Cassady and the Merry Pranksters were on the road in their magic bus they named Further — dropping acid and undermining the status quo in their way.

Magazines like *Ramparts* began showing up in Taft mailboxes. There appeared to be a showdown coming. Anyone with an inkling of what was happening in America could see it was a powder keg. Hard-hat construction workers had bumper stickers that read "America: Love It or Leave It." VW vans and bugs answered back with "America: Change It or Lose It." Battle lines between pro-war and antiwar, black and white, rich and poor were shaping up with skirmishes already taking place.

If Taft had been printing bumper stickers, I can think of a few that would have expressed its position on current events: "Meso-potamia: Love It or Leave It;" "Cosines: Learn Them or Lose Them;" "Go Big Red." In all seriousness, Taft did take a strong position on one trend on college campuses: Under no circum-stances would protests, sit-ins or any other demonstrations be tolerated on campus. We were told "keep your head, while all about you are losing theirs," and reminded how privileged we were. In Mr. Esty's speeches, we were the leaders of tomorrow. How we'd become the leaders of tomorrow by being kept in the dark *today* was a palliative, I suppose, that only the truly faithful at Taft could swallow.

I looked forward to movie night every Saturday night and on holidays. The screen in Bingham Auditorium was as large as any city theater's; the seats plush velvet and the films first run. There was no need to go off campus to see a movie — the same as for most everything else. The only movies I can recall that year were *The Heart is the Lonely Hunter*, *A Man for All Seasons* and perhaps *A Lion in Winter*. My rating system was quite simple. Any that showed a skirt above a knee was a masterpiece. I had no issue with the movies themselves. They were a welcome escape from our exile at Taft. But there were never follow-up discussions about these movies — either at vespers or in the classroom.

I wondered what film directors and screenwriters would make of a place like Taft. Some of the best movies made in the 1960s were decidedly anti-authoritarian, and the heroes (or anti-heroes) were generally in conflict with some repressive government or powerful authority bent on suppressing new ideas or individu-als that threatened to upend the established order. They often mirrored the cultural zeitgeist taking place in America. But like Mr. Marx after we watched *The Lord of the Flies*, there was mostly dead silence after the curtain went down following the movies.

At vespers, Mr. Zaeder, our chaplain, continued to preach the benefits of faith and religion. Walking down the hall to dinner after vespers, a small knot of students would follow, peppering him with questions. The same went for Mr. Esty. They both

Taft chaplain Mr. Zaeder

basked in the attention and rightly so. Taft didn't need a Third Wise Man to guide us to the manger. We had the two of them.

Students were required to attend church only three Sundays a year. But one of those scheduled Sundays happened to be the same day as Super Bowl III — Broadway Joe Namath and the Jets versus old-school, high-top-shoed Johnny Unitas and the heavily favored Baltimore Colts. It was one of the most highly anticipated football games ever. For many Taft students from New York City, church that day was a special disappointment. Why that day and time were chosen was anyone's guess, although I doubt God had anything to do with it. The service took place during the middle of the game, and there was another fifteen-minute penalty walk-off over and back from school. It wasn't the Los Angeles Rams playing, so truthfully, I didn't care if I missed the game.

In the middle of the sermon, a huge cheer broke out. It stopped the pastor in his tracks. He looked around, completely gob smacked. I didn't know what was happening either. I was just glad it wasn't me in the spotlight trying to figure it out. I could see he remained dumbfounded, even as the cheers began to die down. When all eyes were on him again, his bewilderment soft-ened to a lost, rapturous smile. Like either he'd said something so profound it merited remembering for next Sunday — or else he had an epiphany, along the lines of Jesus stiff-arming Lucifer on his way to the end zone. I was starting to silently root for the man. After a minute or two he gathered himself and carried on — blessedly unaware that half the students were listening to the game on transistor radios plugged into their ears.

Not long after, I was awakened from a deep sleep one night when my light snapped on. I opened my eyes and before I could register what was happening, Mr. Marx was standing over me in his pajamas and said in a matter-of-fact way, "You're giving me a back rub." I blinked several times trying to comprehend what he just said. "Get up," he demanded, "You're giving me a back rub." I had no idea what was going on — just a sick feeling. "Get up," he repeated, "Stop wasting time." He took off his pajama tops and threw them on top of Chip's old bed. Then he yanked my blankets off.

I was in a fog, as though I'd woken up after dozing through the first half of a movie. I didn't know what was happening. But I could tell he meant business. That this was serious. I kept thinking this can't be real. He can't ask me to do something like that. And he certainly can't make me. Where was Mr. Esty? He wasn't there my first night, but perhaps he'd be my Johnny on the Spot now and save the day. I stalled, waiting for the sound of footsteps coming to my rescue. In movies, the cavalry always came. Just when you gave up hope and thought they wouldn't. Only not this time.

Aside from the first night, Mr. Marx had never come into my room after lights out. This was breaking our treaty, our proto-col, our traditions, not to mention the arrangement we had and the boundaries we'd established. We had sort of a truce. Or so I believed. That was one of my mother's favorite words, truce. Probably with roots in Latin or Greek. Whenever I had a fight with another kid growing up, she'd trot that word out and make us shake hands. Well, a truce was no help to me now. I was just starting to get some of my old confidence back. A belief in myself that he'd been chipping away at ever since I'd arrived. Why would he do this to me now?

Of course, Mr. Marx didn't see it that way. I could tell by the look on his face. He looked at me as though I were responsible. Like I'd triggered him, but he was already past that. He was wagering that the fear he'd instilled in me the first night would come back. And he bet right because my fear came back in spades. I was afraid he would hit me again if I refused. I felt myself crumple when I realized I didn't have the power to stop him. And then came the stark clarity of how Taft's motto *Not to be served, but to serve* was about to play out for me. I no longer had to guess what he meant when he said I was "probably at Taft for other reasons." The reason was quite clear now. I was an ungrateful servant taking up space in a hallowed school that cherished the good old days of ancient Greece and Rome almost as much as he did. My parents were rich enough to send me there, which he would have resented, while all I had to offer *his* Taft was a nubile adolescent body sprinkled with some spirited resistance. Resistance that was about to undergo a reality check. I got out of my bed, half believing that I owed him for putting up with me for as long as he had. I was there to serve. He was my master, to be served. A debt owed. A debt to collect. A private lesson for me to learn. It was as simple, and twisted, as that.

He lay face down on Chip's old bed and ordered me to get on top of him. I did as I was told. I made a conscious effort to separate my mind from my body. Something that proved easier said than done. I wanted to get it over with as quickly as I could. I started up at the shoulders, nauseated by the feel of his bare skin. His body odor was strong; his face was buried in Chip's old pillow. Both his hands were underneath him. He issued muffled commands. "Harder" then "lower."

He let out little grunts of satisfaction when I was doing it right. I alternated between kneading the muscles under his doughy skin with little karate chops and soft circular scratches with my fingernails, trying to remember what the counselor at Bob Mathias's camp had liked years earlier. The word I dreaded but kept hearing was "lower" but I knew he wouldn't leave unless I did as I was told. At last, working on his lower back just above his waist, I was almost home free. I'd given him a good massage for an amateur. He had no reason to complain. At that point he began to spasm and let out several satisfied grunts, letting me know that I was finally doing it right.

By then the smell in my room was so strong I had to breathe through my mouth. The room felt like a sauna. I was kneading his lower back as hard as I could, the sweat dripped off my forehead, stinging my eyes. I turned my head sideways to try to get the image of his body underneath me out of my mind when I saw my reflection in the fogged window. I was sitting astride him in my boxer shorts. I looked like a jockey — an image that burned permanently into my memory.

"Off!" he said at last, and just in case I hadn't heard, he bucked. I climbed off. He got up and leered at me with a pleased, spent look. I could see the large bulge in his pajamas. His parting words to me were "Don't be such a prude." He put his pajama top back on and then before leaving, glared at me, daring me to do something about it. I just kept staring at the floor. That told him all he needed to know.

Oddly enough, I did not sleep tight that night. His smell permeated the room, but it was not nearly as bad as the stench of my own cowardice. I tried thinking about other things. The polka dot bikini girl. Searching for hot sand with Preston on Santa Monica State Beach. The Band. Beer signs. Revere Teens dances. Anything I could and nothing helped. My mind kept coming back to that image of me in the window. Why didn't I have the courage to stand up to him? You're a coward, my conscience answered back. Now what?

I'd been forced to swallow my pride before, but not like this. I needed someone to blame other than myself. I tried focusing on Mr. Marx, but what was he *really*? He was just a sick person I had no control over. Who put him in control of me? My parents. *Paying* him to do this to me. For several hours, I could not get that out of my head. They were *paying* Mr. Marx, *and Taft*, to do this to me.

As the thought repeated itself that night, I became aware of what sounded like someone breathing in my ear. I don't know what came first. My begging for God to help me, or the sound of His breathing in my ear. Either way, it was the first bit of comfort I had in several hours and I began to calm down. I had reasoned everything out. My parents weren't going to help. *They sent me here.* Mr. Esty wasn't going to help. *His school not only hired him, but also put me in a distant tower across the hall from this man.* So, had God finally arrived to my rescue? Had He put me through some ultimate test of faith to let me know He existed? I kept listening to God's steady breath in my ear, telling me that everything would turn out all right. I finally fell asleep with that thought whispering in my ear.

The following night I heard the breathing in my ear again. Only this time I realized it wasn't God. It was just the sound of my pulse in my ear pressed against the pillow. If there was any silver lining it was this: along with my parents, I could count out God and miracles to save me. I was officially on my own.

I may have been forced to give Mr. Marx one or two more "back rubs" over the next two or three weeks. I can't say for sure because it was something I had to put out of my mind if I was going to survive. I can still recall seeing the shadow of his shoes under the threshold of my door late at night and the anxiety it brought. I knew that after the first one he had broken my will to stop him. That ate away at me. Worse, I was now an active participant in his perversions — all because I'd failed to fight back. I could come forward with accusations. But to whom? And what would the consequences be?

If I told Bruce, he might become suspicious. I could not afford to risk losing the only close friend I had at Taft, or open myself up to wild rumors if he told someone else.

If I told Mr. Esty, it would be my word against Mr. Marx's. I would have to admit I'd given him back rubs and, like the golden calf in The Band's *To Kingdom Come*, that would point the finger right back at me. If I dropped out of Taft, I would have to go back to Greenwich and face my parents. I knew what they would think. I'd gotten involved in something tawdry and was probably at least partly to blame, given their blind faith in teachers. We would have to make up a story that wouldn't be believed no matter how we framed it. Finally, I'd be forced to lie to new classmates about why I was changing schools in the middle of the year. If I didn't fully understand what *Catch-22* was about (another Bingham Auditorium movie that year), or what a Hobson's choice was, I did now. I was *living* it.

Winter dragged on toward spring and Easter break. My father arranged a ski trip to Sun Valley, Idaho, along with his best friend

I intentionally turned away from the camera in my class photo

from Middlebury, Mr. Sperry, and his two sons, Allan and Ben. Young Allan was my age and had been one of my best friends growing up in Middlebury. He may have been at Hotchkiss but we'd lost track of each other long ago. Ben was a couple of years younger. Either right before or after that trip, we took our lower mid class picture at Taft. It was a cold winter's day and we were all gathered outside in front of the school. I turned my face away from the photographer in protest.

I've retained very few memories of that ski trip but one stands out. Sun Valley was warm, the sky was deep blue, and the snow was granular and very easy to ski on. World-famous Leif Erickson was Sun Valley's director of skiing and I secretly hoped he'd catch a glimpse of me hot-dogging and recruit me onto the junior Olympic team. That would provide the perfect excuse for leaving Taft. With that in mind, I bombed down the intermediate runs and vadeled on the flats, hoping he'd notice. I was oblivious to everything except for that.

On one of those runs I accidently skied into my father and knocked him over. I kept right on going. My father showed up at dinner that evening with a cast on his hand. I'd broken his thumb. I did not offer up much of an apology. As far as I was concerned, he was just another mediocre recreational skier who'd gotten in my way while I was skiing at the out limits of control to make myself into something better. Earlier that same afternoon, another skier did the same thing to me. I didn't connect the dots until later: the man who ran into me had seen what I'd done to my father and given me a dose of my own medicine. That was just war on the slopes as far as I was concerned. The trip did nothing to bring us closer together. If anything, it cemented our differences. If I was an ungrateful brat — well look no further than my father for how I came to be that way.

After spring break, the seniors at Taft were in a celebratory mood. Their academic careers at Taft were essentially over. Their college applications were complete and they were only waiting for letters of acceptance. Before the mail arrived in the PO boxes each morning, they would be milling around. When the envelopes were thick, they whooped it up in ecstasy. When they were thin, you could read the rejection on their faces. The seniors dressed more casually in the spring — Bermuda shorts and sockless loafers. If they didn't show up for vespers or class, there were no repercussions. Most of them continued to follow the rules as a matter of course and conditioning, but unlike the rest of us, their summer vacation had already begun.

I got a new roommate — Richard Bixby, the Georgia boy with the expensive electric guitar that he guarded so fiercely. He asked if he could move in with me. We were not friends, but I agreed to the arrangement. I'd underestimated the danger of not having a buffer against Mr. Marx. The first morning after Bixby moved in, he didn't get out of bed when the rising bell rang. When I returned from breakfast, he was still in bed. When I got back from work schedule after the second recitation (class) he was *still* in bed. When I got back before lunch he was lounging around in his bathrobe and slippers. I liked his style but it turned out that he wasn't protesting against Taft.

If my recollection is correct, Bixby and his father were flying back to Taft after Christmas break when his father, seated next to him, suffered a heart attack. I don't know what kind of relationship they had, only that as a southern boy, Richard was already a fish out of water at Taft. His father's death seemed to extinguish any last reason for him to be there.

If there was ever a time for a master or someone like Mr. Esty, Mr. Zaeder or his adviser to step up and help him recover emotionally, this was it. I recall there was some minimal effort in that regard, but whatever was said didn't work. Bixby continued to live at the Taft Inn until checkout time, just a few weeks after he'd moved in with me. He gave me his father's surgical scissors before he left as a parting gift for letting him room with me. I still have the scissors and sometimes think of him when I use them. I never saw or heard from him again. Bixby was another reminder that Taft was a sink or swim institution. Where adult understanding for boys in need of help was in short supply.

By then the snow had long since melted and the trees on Taft's campus were starting to bud. Even with the valve closed, the steam radiator in my room put out so much heat I had to keep both my windows open during the day. I was going to try out for the lower school tennis team when I found out that Mr. Gould, the basketball coach, would be in charge. I decided to lay low and enjoy as much after-class free time as possible. I still enjoyed athletics, but the coaches of organized sports at Taft had sapped nearly all the fun out of them for me.

Mr. Marx's winter aggression subsided. After Bixby left, Mr. Marx's visits to my room didn't tick back up like I thought they might. I was grateful, of course. I only wish he'd gotten the message back in September. Still, it was strange to see such a change in him. What he was doing became more obvious as the next few weeks went by. He was avoiding me.

He did remind me that he still owed my parents one more letter, and that I would have to apply myself much harder if I was going to turn things around the following year. One afternoon he read me a rough draft of the final letter he was writing. It was similar to the first two he wrote. They all followed the same script:

> Jack is a great kid. I like him personally. He has shown some growth and maturity.... However... In these other areas... he needs to show... greater improvement.... While I still believe Jack is not living up to his full potential at Taft, if he applies himself next year.... Sincerely, Mr. Walter Marx.

CHAPTER 15

The roofs at school were all pointed, steep and made of slate. Or so I thought. There were some hips and valleys of rolled asphalt that one could not see from below. There happened to be one outside of Mr. Marx's bedroom window that he told me about; one with a flat spot, large enough to recline and sunbathe. On one of the first really warm days in late spring, Mr. Marx said I could come over and use it while he was out. I was surprised he made the offer after ignoring me for weeks. I still didn't trust him, but he left his door open and went out for one of his long strolls with Argus, which usually lasted a couple of hours. The temptation of lounging in the sun after a long cold winter that left me pale as a ghost was too much. I had on a pair of shorts and took off my t-shirt and basked in the sun. After the first or second tanning session, I heard him arrive back earlier than usual. As I climbed in through his window, he came into his bedroom. I can't remember whether he closed the door or not, but he had his trademark leer, which I knew meant trouble.

He walked over from the door to the far side of the bed. I edged toward the door. I was no longer cornered, so for the moment I felt safe. Out of the blue, he asked me if I knew anything about French whores. While I was trying to absorb that question, he unzipped his fly, pulled out his thing, and then began to describe in clinical detail what "French whores had done to it." I just stood there, mildly fazed at this point in our relationship. With the word "whore" sounding exactly like "horror," my mind flashed to a seedy brothel, and a small room lined with red velvet wallpaper that smelled of desperation and cheap perfume. Even in a place like that, I could not imagine how any woman could bear to touch him. He was untouchable. His personality left something to be desired, too. I left him in mid-sentence, which was probably how his French "social worker" left him when his time was up. He may have been hoping for one last teachable moment with me. Mr. Marx was a teacher right to the end. If he had one redeeming quality, I guess you could say he never entirely gave up on me. Hard to say what was going through his mind, but there was no mistaking the jilted expression on his face as I turned to go. As though the last friend he had in the world had just walked out on him.

As much as I wanted good marks, at least good enough to keep me out of study hall, I wasn't inspired to cheat. Giving a teacher the satisfaction of thinking I cared that much had a lot to do with it. For every test or paper turned in at Taft, students had to sign a pledge at the bottom that they hadn't given or received any aid. If they did and were caught, it was grounds for immediate dismissal. I did not see any wholesale cheating when I was there. The humiliation of getting caught and the consequences of getting kicked out were too great. Although I'll admit that hearing about one method involving a rubber band stretched between a collar button down to the palm with the answers attached did strike me as ingenious. When the teacher told you to open your hand, your cheat sheet would retract up your sleeve and disappear. That I might have tried in engineering class, if only Taft offered one.

Drugs — mainly marijuana, but also amphetamines, alcohol, psychedelics, even cough syrup — became the main coping mechanisms for dealing with the pressure to succeed. As the school year progressed, Mr. Esty's vespers' speeches began to zero in on this issue. His remedy for students getting illegally high was to get "naturally high" instead. This led students to form the "Natural High Society," which began to rival the BFD movement in popularity. I was not into drugs. I'd had enough bad trips at Taft already. I also wanted to remember everything that was happening — almost as much as I wanted to forget.

On one particularly pleasant spring afternoon I saw some seniors kicking a soccer ball around on the lawn below Woody's window. I decided to join in. After the game, Victor "Vic" Rocha, one of the stars of the varsity, showed me how to take the ball between my feet, slide it up the back of my heel and flick it up in the air over my head. Victor would seem to live up to Taft's promise of nurturing "tomorrow's leaders" by becoming the U.S. ambassador to Bolivia in 2000 and then serving as an advisor to Southern Command of the US military from 2006-2012. He was arrested by the FBI in 2023 – accused of spying for Cuba against the US for over 30 years. He may not have ended up the type of success story Taft hoped when they spotlighted him in a 2004 *Alumni Bulletin* story, but I'll always remember him as a wizard with the ball who taught me with patience and kindness. That is one of my best memories of Taft. It was soon to be followed by one of my worst. An evening that would change the course of my life forever.

I'd earned a stayover at the end of the year. I don't remember what for. Setting off some firecrackers up near the Wade House comes to mind. Either way, I was on bounds at the end of the year. I would have to remain and do some menial chores before I was excused to go home. Senior graduation was scheduled after the regular school year ended, so my stayover coincided with their graduation. Another sign of how bad things were was that I was as resigned to staying over as I was about going home.

I made my way up to Woody's room after dinner. There were rumors of a party. When I got there, it was bedlam. I think every senior at Taft was at ISP that night. There wasn't a master in sight, even though they were all still there for graduation and end-of-year student reviews. The air was thick with smoke and incense, and the stereo was so loud that you had to shout to be heard by the person next to you. I wasn't sure I'd be welcome as a lower mid but I acted as though I belonged. A few seniors gave me *the look*, but most didn't seem to care. They were there for one last blowout and if I happened to be there — and Woody was cool with it — so be it. Most were looking over the top of my head anyway — to a much brighter future than mine.

It was either Schuyler Gould or George Turner who flashed me a pint of Smirnoff vodka from inside their overcoat and offered it for sale. I fished into my pocket and forked over $5, reasoning that no one there deserved a drink more than I did. I also wanted to impress the seniors that I could hold my own. I could either party with them or slink back to my room and spend my last quiet evening at Taft alone, with Mr. Marx across the hall.

The first swig evaporated halfway down my throat and left a burning vapor trail in its wake. Prior to that, my experience with alcohol had been limited to drinking half a beer at David Schiff's house one night over the course of several hours. "Are you drunk?" David's older brother asked me as I stared into space. With all the effort I'd put in I'd certainly hoped so, but the fact was I didn't like the taste of alcohol. I also didn't want to grow up and do the things adults did to cope with the stupid situations they put themselves in. Which was what I was about to do.

By that point, my inability to chart my own course after giving up on my parents to chart it for me hadn't gone so swell. The bottle in my hand seemed as good a way as any to escape that feeling, if only for a little while, and celebrate what I thought was the end of a long nightmare. I forced myself to take another pull and then another and another. The last third went down quite easily. I polished off the pint in about twenty minutes.

I felt extremely happy, and mature beyond my years. I took a few drags from a cigarette for good measure. I was taking it all in, feeling very grown up and more than holding my own until the room began to spin. I tried closing my eyes but the black and red speckled universe spun ever faster. I was having trouble standing. I was unable to maintain, and when my condition became apparent, a group of seniors knotted around me.

There was a short discussion about what to do. I had trouble following most of it. All I wanted was to go back to my room and sleep it off. The spinning was getting worse. I was hoping Woody would help me back, but it was another senior, a member of Mr. Wynne's varsity wrestling team, who volunteered instead. I was embarrassed, but in no shape to argue, or to get back on my own.

Russell Pais somehow got me to my room. I thanked him and collapsed on my bed. He turned off the light and I thought he was going to leave and that would be that. And then he did something that even in my semi-coherent state I remember thinking was odd. Instead of leaving, he pulled up a chair and sat next to me in the dark, without a word. He just sat there looking at me from no more than a foot away. If it had been Woody, I would have understood it, but I did not know Russell and I thought it extraordinary that he would sit there with me

1968 senior monitors

instead of going back to the party. More than extraordinary. I drifted in and out of consciousness, but each time I opened my eyes to check, he was still there. At first, I thought he was just overly concerned about me, but then it started to seem weird. I asked him several times to go back to the party. What was happening to me was something I wanted to deal with on my own, and now that I was safely back in my own bed, I could begin to repair the damage I'd done. What happened after I passed out for good that night remains a mystery.

In the morning, I heard voices. They sounded like a mob coming up a hill with pitchforks and torches to do away with me. They grew louder and angrier, until I came to recognize they were one and the same, and the voice was a sadly familiar one. I opened one eye and saw Mr. Marx standing over my bed, spouting gibberish. The room was still spinning, more slowly now, but enough to realize I was still in bad shape. Daylight was streaming through the window. My mouth was parched, my head throbbed and the light hurt my eyes, so I closed them again. My condition did not seem to rattle Mr. Marx. I tried tuning him out but he kept ranting on about something, making it difficult for me to go back to sleep. I presumed it had to do with my bender the night before and I didn't need him to remind me of that.

My parents were coming to get me in a few hours and I had to start thinking about how I was going to manage both packing and sobering up. Mr. Marx seemed the least of my worries. Then I began piecing together certain things he was repeating over and over, and realized my drunkenness had nothing to do with it. "Caught you in bed last night with..." "You had a big smile on your face..." "You can't wash off VD, Coe...."

He finally left, slamming the door behind him. I drifted back to unconsciousness but that didn't stop me from trying to untangle what Mr. Marx had said. Silent alarms began to go off. Had Russell Pais done something after I passed out? The unnerving feeling I had about him seated next to my bed came back to me. I told myself it wasn't possible. A senior wouldn't do that. Besides, Russell was a known straight-arrow, and a senior class committee member. Why would he be even remotely interested in someone like me?

But I knew Mr. Marx wasn't entirely lying because he mentioned Russell by name. Or did he? I think so. But had he merely seen Russell sitting next to me in the chair, or actually *in my bed with me*? I racked my brain for any sensation or memory after passing out. Nothing.

A new wave of worry crested over me. Would Mr. Marx tell my parents? Was he downstairs telling Mr. Esty or Mr. Oscarson right now? Did he tell me he'd taken a photograph, or was I only imagining that? If I was confronted, what story was I going tell? What could I say that wouldn't implicate me? If I accused Mr. Marx of the things he'd done all year, all he had to do was point to my drunken orgy the night before. As for the drunken part, there was no denying that.

Part of me felt like giving up, staying in bed and going back to the dream I was having. Waiting for the mob to arrive and put me out of my misery. That seemed like a pretty good dream to hold onto.

The only thing that got me out of bed that morning was the specter of more people coming into my room to check on me. What staggered me when I did get up was the amount of vomit. There were brown lakes of it all over my bed and all over the floor — enough to make me wonder if some of my internal organs weren't part of the mix. Trying not to step in any of it, I made the woozy walk down the hall, took a shower, and began the long process of cleaning up the mess.

The rest of that day is a blur. I have no recollection of seeing Mr. Marx after that. My parents, or perhaps it was just my mother, came to pick me up later that morning or afternoon. I was still drunk, on top of a stump-splitting headache. I told her I wasn't feeling well and slept all the way back to Greenwich. I slept for the better part of three days until my hangover finally wore off. I don't think my mother and father had any clue what was wrong. They never asked and for the most part left me alone. By my third day home, I was beginning to feel better and sitting up in bed. To cheer me up, my mother brought the newly arrived *Sports Illustrated* up to my room. I'd always enjoyed reading *Sports Illustrated* but there was something about the cover of this one that spoke directly to me. It was a picture of Joe Namath, the Jets' Super Bowl hero, slumped in front of several microphones. He was facing a career-ending scandal for being part owner of a New York nightclub, the Three Bachelors, with apparent ties to the mob. The headline: "Namath Weeps."

PART 5

In Search of the Lost Chord

CHAPTER 16

I believe one reason my parents left me in my room relatively unmolested for three straight days was that they had
more fun and games in store for me. They'd signed me up
for another summer camp experience. Facing the alternative
of spending another summer with my parents in Greenwich, I
accepted the lesser of two evils and agreed to go to Bart Strang's
ranch in Carbondale, Colorado. Mr. Strang was a Taft alumnus
and evidently my parents thought the more immersed I was
in Taft culture, the better. I left in late June and found myself
in a bunkhouse full of boys my age from various eastern prep
schools. None were from Taft. There was also a girls' bunkhouse.
A girl I'd known from my early Middlebury days, Andy Lilly,
was also there.

It was billed as a working ranch. We were tasked with building
pens for cows and horses under the guidance of the ranch foreman and several counselors in their early twenties. The foreman
was fond of repeating this cheery bromide regarding the girls
in camp: "Old enough to bleed — old enough to butcher." One

counselor, a drugstore cowboy named Rugger, particularly stood out in his leather chaps and red and white bandana beautifully stuffed into his snap-button western shirt.

After being quarantined for the better part of a year, I was starving for female attention but unsure how to go about it. Another boy and I finally came up with a ruse. We billed ourselves as psychologists and offered our services to any girl who wanted to be psychoanalyzed. A surprising number did, and we began squeezing them into our busy afternoon schedule. We would start by getting them to open up about their parents and how they were making their lives miserable by not letting them do the things they wanted. Some of them, like Andy Lilly, were quite attractive, and we would doodle their figures in our notepads as we listened; daydreaming unprofessional thoughts as their

With a fellow camper at the Strang Hereford ranch in Carbondale, Colorado, July 1969.

innermost feelings poured out. We were coming at them from a different angle than most boys. This caught them off guard, but their feelings got so out of hand that we couldn't capitalize on their misery. Being two untrained quacks meant all of our sessions ended with them breaking down in tears. And yet, they kept asking for more.

There were a couple of girls who seemed interested in me, but the closest I ever got to one was an awkward kiss while listening to Zager and Evans "In the Year 2525" one afternoon on a couch. On the evening of July 20, 1969, we all gathered around a black and white television after dinner and watched the grainy image of Neil Armstrong stepping onto the moon. That very same moon was bright and clear when we went outside to check on it that night, but it seemed a little less mysterious.

I spent most evenings after lights out indulging quietly in the only pleasure I knew before being able to go to sleep. My memories of what happened at Bob Mathias's Sierra Boy's camp were still fresh. As much as I found it hard to believe that others in the bunkhouse weren't equally inclined, I did not want to go through that again. Afterward I felt gross, dirty and ashamed as usual, but Mr. Happy had a mind of his own and there was nothing I could do once it was made up.

Early on, one night shortly after lights out, the door to the bunkhouse opened and Rugger led in a new boy who had arrived late. The boy introduced himself with a big, hearty Texas drawl and went to his bunk to settle in. He was as big as his voice and wore a ten-gallon hat, but he had no idea what he was walking into and neither did I. Shortly after the lights went out, someone said something nasty to him. He did not respond and that led to another insult and then another, until the insults took on a life of their own. In the dark, where no one could see where they were coming from. It went on like that for over an hour. A complete verbal beatdown that I'll never forget. It reminded me of Dwight Ely, the whipping boy Taft seniors regularly dumped on to make themselves feel better. For all the claims prep schools made about instilling high moral character — turning out fine young cannibals would be closer to the truth.

I received a letter from my parents my third or fourth week. They told me we were moving back to California and would pick me up before the session ended. That was a pleasant shock. The bit in my mouth was jerked yet again. But at least this time I was homeward bound. Part of me wondered when my parents would just admit we were Bedouins, and their search for a permanent home would never end. As we were leaving, Mr. Strang handed them a note about his impressions of me. Just as with Mr. Marx's letters home, my parents deserved to know how I was behaving when they weren't around. Mr. Strang may have said something nice about my hard work although I rarely saw him except at meals, when the lighthearted bickering between him and his wife was part of the after-dinner entertainment. I heard they divorced not long after. In the note he called me the "Sigmund Freud of the Rocky Mountains." My mother thought that was cute and asked me what it meant. My father just stared ahead, gripping the steering wheel with both hands, keeping his thoughts to himself as we got onto I-70 and headed west.

I made it clear to my parents that there was no way I was going back to Taft in the fall. Prep school was a bust and because their own East Coast plans went bust too, they didn't press the matter. They'd bought a house in Brentwood, not far from where we lived before. My older sister was going to UCLA and dating a track star who had blown out his knee. He was in the process of reinventing himself as a computer scientist. My other sister was going to USC and hanging out with the in-crowd, including members of the football team, in a defiant shift toward interracial dating that my father was determined to block.

For my part, I wanted to get back to my old life. I'd miss Bruce, Woody, John Dant and a few others at Taft, but on the whole my experience there was so bad that all I wanted was to chalk it up to a lesson learned and move on.

I tried reconnecting with my old California friends like nothing had happened in my year away. It wasn't easy. I felt like a new kid on the block who had to get to know everyone all over again. Sometimes I felt paranoid around my friends, believing they sometimes looked at me like I might have carried back with me an infectious disease.

I spent a lot of time that summer with my old best friend, Preston, going to the beach, body surfing, searching for hot sand and listening to music. I turned Preston onto The Band and showed him how to make paper airplanes, but those were about the only things I had to offer. Preston's blond hair was down to his shoulders — something his permissive parents allowed while I was still pulling mine after a mandatory haircut to make it grow back faster. He was still Preston and one of the more popular and best-looking boys in school, but I noticed he'd become quieter and more introspective. I never would find out what brought about this change. Too much time had passed. We still connected over music and our favorite TV shows. But while I didn't trust my parents anymore, Preston seemed to trust his. They were far more liberal and relaxed than mine.

Hanging out with girls at the beach was a great way to pass the time, but also a reminder of what I'd missed and how much I'd changed. Coming from a high-wattage school like Taft back to an environment that was even more laid-back than I'd remembered was a bit of a let-down. I missed the adrenaline rush of sneaking out of my room and the stairwell smoking sessions. When I wasn't hanging out with friends, I played guitar, listened to music and read — always with an eye out for a better way of life.

I went out for the Palisades High "B" football team that September but dropped out after "hell week" before the season started. In many ways it was a repeat of my experience at Taft. Eleventh graders who didn't move up to the junior varsity or varsity squads were bigger and cemented their stature with the coaches by forming cliques that relegated most tenth graders like me to second-string linemen and practice fodder. My decision to quit was also partly due to one of the coaches, Mr. Enstedt, who seemed to have more than a passing interest in me as well as many of the boys in school. His invitations to come over to his house after class "to be photographed" were well known to everyone except, I suppose, the administration.

Aside from football, PaliHi was a welcome relief from Taft. In addition to regular studies, there were several vocational classes, like wood and auto shop. The homework load was light and while most of the teachers were competent, they also seemed to understand that there were things outside their classroom that were just as important to our development. I had a white teacher for African American studies, a black teacher for English, and a teacher from the deep South who taught Civil War history from the Confederate point of view. After school I had time to watch television, play pickup basketball games, play mud football during a rainstorm, or Dibble Dabble — a swimming pool game that involved placing a small twig down by the drain. As it rises, everyone jumps in to try to snatch it.

It wasn't all fun and games. Several of us were finally roped into attending cotillion every other Friday evening at the Bel-Air Bay Club, making a grinding start to the weekend. The matron who ran it was forever promising that her nephew (or son) Jethro, the star of the popular TV show *Beverly Hillbillies*, would come the following week. Which he never did.

We left Greenwich because my father quit Anaconda Brass and Copper, where he had worked for twenty-four years, one year short of qualifying for a pension. Part of that had to do with the nationalization of Anaconda's copper mines in Chile. Anaconda's gravy train of cheap copper ore came to an end after Allende was elected. My father went to work for a financial service company, Seaboard, in Beverly Hills. An acquaintance, who was a lawyer for Seaboard, got him the job. My father did not discuss his new job with me, or if he did, it went in one ear and out the other. The president of the firm, Mr. Brinkerhoff, showed up at our house one evening in a chauffeur-driven Bentley with his platinum blond wife to take my parents out to dinner. He was a caricature of a Republican fat cat right down to his jowls that moved up and down like a pufferfish when he spoke. I was disappointed though not surprised that my parents would associate with people like that. My father's blind trust in Seaboard would soon be shattered, and he'd be facing a nightmare of his own over the next two years.

I was getting ready for school one morning when on my Seagram's 7 clock radio I heard the lead news story about a fraud indictment handed down by the Securities and Exchange Commission. I was not paying much attention until I heard my father's name.

I was stunned. As much as I felt distanced from my father, I always knew he was a decent, honest man without a criminal bone in his body. How could this be possible? I was highly embarrassed and cringed at the thought of going to school. I made it through the day and the rest of the week with my head held low. No one said a word to me about the news but for a long time I wondered who else had heard and what was being said behind my back.

This was something my father could not keep from us. Turns out, his lawyer friend at Seaboard had asked my father to sign a document without bothering to read it. That document defrauded an investor out of $100,000, and my father had a judgment levied against him. On top of that, the SEC filed several criminal complaints against several of the firm's officers, including my father. As this was unfolding, he started going to business school at night. He was 50 years old and decided he wanted to own his own business. A business broker recommended a small boiler manufacturing company for sale in Downey — close to where he had previously worked in Paramount in his Anaconda days. My father knew nothing about boilers but he did have a natural understanding of mechanical things and reasoned that steam and hot water would always be in demand. He borrowed money from my mother and gave me and my sisters shares of stock in return for the cash we had in our savings accounts.

The boiler company turned out to have a lot of bad inventory — steel that was cut the wrong size and was basically scrap. Making matters worse, the former owner had burned a lot of bridges before he sold the company. Several customers used the change in ownership as an excuse to switch their business over to his competitors. The former owner (and one of his partners who owned the building my father leased) thought my father would go broke in a year or two and they would buy the company back for pennies on the dollar. My father's way of dealing with all these headwinds was to throw up every morning before heading off to work.

These facts came out slowly over time. He may have been more tight-lipped than usual on Monday mornings, but he somehow maintained his sense of humor, an interest in his children and his way of making wry observations of the world at large. He liked reading Sunday editorials in the *LA Times* to us (at the head of the table over coffee in his bathrobe) that either "frosted his ass" or "said it better" than he could. He often worked six days a week and sometimes seven. On weekends he would go over the company books in the morning and spend the afternoon outdoors, planting and moving shrubs around the garden at my mother's direction. After numerous depositions, the SEC lawyers dropped the criminal charge against my father. I called him "Daddy Lawbuster" after that and we all thought it was pretty funny because he was about as law-abiding as he could be, dating to his Middlebury days when he was a deputy sheriff. He still carried the badge in his wallet. He was also still on the hook for the judgment, though, and didn't have the money to pay it off. My grandfather stepped in and settled the judgment; my father promised to pay him back after the boiler company turned a profit. It would be a long, hard road before he turned the company around.

Years later, we were driving home one night and he told me, "Well I've got some good news. We only lost ten thousand dollars this month." At first, I thought he was joking. Then I could see he wasn't and a light went on in my head: I had a lot to learn about life and business, and there was something to admire in a man who could face that kind of reality with that kind of attitude. We finally had something in common: a couple of underdogs fighting uphill battles of our own.

In our family, money and affection went together. Twice a year, cash or a check was enclosed in a Christmas or birthday card signed "with affection" by my grandparents or "with love" from my parents. The sums were not exorbitant, $25 or $50 — $250 by the time we aged out — and we were encouraged to deposit rather than spend the money. It went unsaid that to remain recipients of these good graces, we were to live up to their expectations — behaving well, making our beds, sitting up straight and getting good grades. Writing a book like this when my parents and grandparents were alive would have earned me a Christmas card calling me a humbug — check not enclosed.

Early in my parents' marriage, their housekeeper, Lucie Andre, mentioned to my mother that she not only washed my grandmother's rags but ironed and folded them too. My mother thought this was funny and mentioned it to some of her friends. In a small town like Middlebury, this got back to my grandmother. My grandparents met my father at a train station a short time later and suggested he divorce my mother. My grandfather held considerable sway over my father's career at Anaconda at the time, and therefore his ability to support his young family. My father told them if they were going to try to force him to make that decision, they weren't going to like the answer. My parents' marriage survived, but it was a lesson I'm sure was not lost on my father. I've no doubt the decision to send me to Taft was heavily influenced by his parents. Once we were back in Connecticut in 1968, he was back in their orbit.

As my father got older, his appreciation for the saying "Most men lead lives of quiet desperation" seemed to deepen. I was never sure if he meant it as a warning to me — or a fact of life that no man escapes. I took it as a warning and was determined not to end up like that. I'd survived Mr. Marx and Taft with my spirits intact and I thought I was stronger for it. All I had to do was get through high school, and then I'd be free to pursue a life that avoided desperation. My father seemed to have forgotten the North Wind stories he read to me as a child. I hadn't. I still wanted to live in a log cabin someday. More than ever in fact. Unlike most of my friends, I'd had a private lesson regarding the dark side of power at Taft, and I would tuck that bit of wisdom in my back pocket and use it to avoid the traps ahead.

My parents' twenty-fifth wedding anniversary was December 14, 1969. They decided to celebrate it in Middlebury, which made sense since many of their oldest and dearest friends still lived

there. Out of a deep love for my mother and his three children, my father decided it would be a wonderful surprise to
fly my sisters and me back there for the weekend. We would be
squirreled away at my grandparents' house until the big gala on
Saturday evening when we would be trotted out to complete the
portrait of a successful marriage and a happy family.

Two newspaper clippings from the *Waterbury Republican* regarding Taft were forwarded by my grandparents shortly before we
left. One involved the passing of a Taft master I didn't know and
the other was about someone I did know — Bill Waldron — the
lower mid who'd been in my history class with Bruce. He'd fallen
through a trap door on the Taft stage. I don't know what effect
my grandparents thought this would have on me. All it did was
remind me how fortunate I was to be back in sunny Southern
California and far away from Taft's dark gravity.

On the Saturday morning after we'd arrived, I made a fateful
decision to go over to Taft and visit my old friends. I had a vision
that Bruce and others would be glad to see me. I'd regained my
color and vitality and wanted to show everyone at Taft what not
being locked up in a prep school looked like. I wanted to prove
that life was, indeed, a thousand times better outside the prison
walls. Instead, the reaction I got floored me. No one seemed
glad to see me. Bruce seemed especially indifferent. I wondered
if it was jealousy and quickly toned down my bragging about
my freedom. But nothing changed as the afternoon wore on.
My reception was lukewarm at best. I was ready to give up and
leave when Bruce mentioned there was a rumor going around
that I might want to know about. I felt my stomach tighten. He

wouldn't tell me what it was. Instead, he directed me to go see an upper mid who might tell me.

I didn't know this upper from my lower mid year — which made what he told me all the more shocking. The rumor was that I'd left Taft because Mr. Marx had caught me in bed with another student. I tried to pass it off as a lie, and then went back to assure Bruce that whatever Mr. Marx said about me wasn't true. We said our goodbyes and I went back to my grandparents to get dressed up for the evening.

I don't believe people choose to be straight or gay any more than they choose their gender, skin color or parents. I can't speak for others, but I don't recall checking off any of those boxes when I

Mr. Marx, consulting with an unidentified student in his role as chairman of the Classics Department.

was in the womb. But in the late 1960s, homosexuality was widely considered deviant. And that was amplified in high school — where boys, some of whom were probably unsure of their own sexual identity, could be particularly brutal to other boys they saw as "different." It wasn't the rumor itself that bothered me. By then I knew I wasn't homosexual, so it was a little like calling me a Venusian. It was the rejection by my friends at Taft that concerned me. My friends weren't narrow minded, but if they believed the rumor, they would have seen me as hiding an important truth from them. They would have seen me as an imposter. And no one likes or trusts an imposter.

That evening I hid the news well but I was devastated. The more I thought it over, the worse it got. I'd just lost my friends at Taft to a rumor and where would the rumor stop? How long before everyone I knew, or used to know in Middlebury, heard the same thing? I'd lived over half my life in Middlebury and I had no way to defend myself from 3,000 miles away. All anyone knew was that I'd left Taft after one year — and now the reason was open to speculation; for reasons that Mr. Marx was only too happy to provide. It was a mind-bender I was going to have to deal with one way or another. As I watched my parents and their friends celebrate that evening, there was only one response I could come up with. I had to make the rumor impossible to believe.

Shortly after we returned to LA, I told my parents I wanted to go back to Taft for my upper mid year. They were delighted. They thought I'd finally come to my senses and understood the value of a good education. I'm sure my grandparents were just as pleased. Getting a better education was the furthest thing from my mind. All I wanted to do was salvage my reputation at Taft and in Middlebury. How to erase the rumor in an all-boys school would be a challenge but what choice did I have? And so began the task. I wrote Bruce and asked if he'd be my roommate if I returned to Taft. I knew I needed him on my side if I was going to pull off what I was planning.

PART 6

A Shiny Light Breaking in the Storm

CHAPTER 17

After returning from the anniversary party, I carried on like everything was normal. I think most of my friends in LA assumed the preppy life was the life for me and I would soon be going back to the East Coast for good.

One of my LA friends was David Newman, an old pal from Canyon Elementary who lived in Rustic Canyon across from Will Rogers State Park. It is one of the prettiest places in all Los Angeles, with creeks and redwoods that make you forget you live in one of the most sprawling, populous cities in America. David's father, Alfred Newman, was one of Hollywood's most acclaimed movie composers. Several Oscar statuettes were scattered about their house in need of a good polish.

David's mother, Martha Newman, was much younger than Alfred and ran the roost that included five children, including David. I overheard she met Mr. Newman when she was a showgirl in Las Vegas. Appearance wise, that didn't surprise me. David was a good athlete and we spent many afternoons shooting hoops in his driveway, followed by dinner and sleepovers. We would watch *Star Trek* before Mrs. Newman would make us get down on our knees and pray before bedtime. Belying her warm southern charm, David's mother was strict about church, school and the music traditions that ran in her husband's family. We would be playing basketball in the driveway and she'd come out and stop the game to make David practice violin for an hour. David's younger brother Tommy would then emerge from the practice room and take over David's spot.

Martha Newman wanted her boys to be well-rounded and that included ski vacations to places like Gstaad, Switzerland. They would return with patches on their parkas to show off all the places they'd been. They knew I loved to ski and invited me to go with them up to Mammoth Mountain in California's Eastern Sierra over Thanksgiving 1969. Having grown up in Connecticut, I had an early start on skiing, beginning in our backyard and then on to places close to home like Catamount, in eastern New York State, about an hour away from our Middlebury home; Jiminy Peak, in western Massachusetts, about two hours away; and finally Mont-Tremblant in Quebec, Canada, about 400 miles north.

David was an avid skier and we would often bus up with our church youth group and ski LA's local mountains on weekends. One afternoon, David and I walked down to his neighbor's house to see if Gary was there. Gary Olson was a year or two behind us, but he was supposedly a good athlete, and we needed him to complete a two-on-two game of hoops. An older blond girl came careening around the corner of their ranch house and practically ran us over with a garden trowel in her hand. She was short and somewhat plump in her blue overalls, but radiant looking — as though she'd just stepped out of a Norwegian travel poster with fjords in the background.

Mrs. Newman and Gary's mother were friends and they planned a family Christmas trip to June Mountain. June was less challenging but you could see Mammoth from the top of it on a clear day. I was invited along as the only outsider. Gary's sister Kristin, the older girl with the trowel, was going, too. Skiing was something I was good at for my age. Maybe the only thing I could take pride in being better at than any of my friends. It also kept me from thinking too much about my upcoming kamikaze mission at Taft.

My middle sister was distancing herself from a boyfriend around that time, Joe Broadhurst, a former member of the University of Denver ski team. He was too independent (or maybe just too wild or uncoachable) to make the US Olympic team and was bumming around western ski resorts like Squaw Valley, Alpine Meadows and Mammoth. By then I had skied with him once or twice. He may have been out of his league when it came to my sister, but he was in a league of his own when it came to skiing.

June was a much smaller and quieter resort than Mammoth with a few mostly beginner and intermediate runs. Gary had never skied before but that didn't stop me from taking him to the top for his first run. I was sure my abilities would rub off on him, but he fell so many times that I gave up. I lapped him several times that morning. To his credit he didn't stab me with his pole or complain when I'd stop to check on him, and he eventually made it down on his own. I liked Gary, but it was a tug of war between helping him learn how to ski and showing off the only skill I felt really good at.

On Sunday, Mrs. Newman piled us all into her car and we went looking for a church to attend morning service. It frustrated me that we were giving up a chance to go skiing on such a perfect morning but I kept my mouth shut as long as I could. I was their guest, after all. When she found the only church in town, she pulled over and squinted at the sign with the service times out front. "Can you read what it says, Coe?" We'd always gotten along well. However, I always had the feeling she suspected I might be a bad influence on David and a little dickens when she wasn't around. She always called me by my last name, perhaps in case her hunch was right. "Closed on Sunday," I replied. I was amused by my little quip, but I don't believe she was.

One evening Joe Broadhurst dropped by. Although he never said anything about it to me, I think he still carried the torch for my sister and I was his last link in that chain. He came from a working-class family in upstate New York, and skiing was maybe his only ticket to a better life. He was a quiet, humble guy who let his skis do the talking — and talk they did. He was a graceful, fearless skier who made me follow him into the trees once — just to show me how much more there was to being a truly great skier than I would ever know. He liked to approach the edge of a steep run lined with expert skiers discussing what fall line to take. Then after awkwardly overshooting the lip, he would make an exaggerated snowplow first turn as if to confirm he'd missed the double black diamond sign and was in over his head. Once he had their attention that an ass-over-teakettle wipeout was about to unfold, he'd deliver a lesson in skiing that left everyone watching slack-jawed as he ripped apart the run, in ways they could only dream of. He had skied with Jean-Claude Killy, winner of all three gold alpine skiing medals at the Grenoble Winter Olympics in 1968 and at that point considered the greatest skier alive. My cachet with the Newman and Olson families went up that evening. Joe brought over the newly released Leslie West album, *Mountain*, which none of us had heard. Along with Leslie West and *Led Zeppelin II*, our nights were spent listening to rock and roll, and our days spent happily on the slopes.

Kristin was the eldest in her family. In addition to Gary (second eldest) she had a younger sister Karinne and a much younger brother, Brigham, who was maybe two or three. Being the eldest, Kristin had natural maternal instincts that made her sweet and protective. I found this an attractive quality. It made me think of my older sisters who more often than not couldn't get them-selves far enough away from me. By the time we got back to Los Angeles, I felt familiar and comfortable enough to go over and visit the Olsons on my own, with or without David.

Preston and I would hitchhike to the Music Odyssey store on Wilshire Boulevard after school every Friday to search the record bins for new releases. At $2.99 an album, we could afford to be experimental, often buying records based on album covers alone, or by scouring the liner notes to see what back-up musicians were listed. This led to some spectacular duds like *Lord Sutch and Heavy Friends* (one of Preston's picks) and *Blue Mountain Eagle* (one of mine), but also some gems like the first albums from the bands Taste and Free.

One cool wet afternoon, I worked up the nerve to walk the two or three miles from my parents' house over to the Olsons with one of my new picks — an album by Zephyr. My pretext was asking Gary if he'd like to listen to it. Gary was out but Kristin was home and invited me in. The album turned out to be not great. The "St. James Infirmary" track was particularly gloomy and not necessarily what you'd play to impress someone you hardly knew. But Kristin seemed happy to have a visitor. After the record was over, she put on a 45 that Gary had recently bought: "Fire" by Arthur Brown. The song was a big AM radio hit at the time, and one of those songs that you could take as either the debut of a serious new artist or a campy cult smash one-hit wonder. After listening to Zephyr, we both took it for the latter and started laughing our heads off.

We played it several times, lip-syncing the song while Brigham stood on his toes, watching us from his crib with eyes almost as big as Kristin's. Kristin may have put on some other albums as the afternoon passed, much like I'd passed other afternoons listening to music with Preston. The rest of her family began to trickle in, and I told her it was probably time for me to go. She invited me to stay for dinner. I hung out with Gary, who'd just returned from a punt, pass and kick competition with his father, while Kristin helped her mother in the kitchen. Their home was filled with loud voices and laughter, except for Mr. Olson who'd retired to his study. Kristin wanted to liven up the mashed potatoes by adding green food coloring, which stirred up a heated debate with her mother in the kitchen. I remained neutral — just happy to be around a family that let everything out instead of holding everything in.

Kristin drove me home after dinner. She was about 18 at the time and a freshman at Colorado College. I knew she was too old and way too attractive to be interested in me, but for whatever reason, she seemed to like my company. Given all the recent strange turns of events in my life, who was I to judge someone out of my league who always seemed happy to see me?

She was still on Christmas break from college when my classes resumed at Palisades High. Sometimes she would pack a picnic basket, pick me up from school at noon, and we'd drive up the coast to Malibu to a little park that overlooked the ocean. I don't think she knew it, but having a girl as pretty as her pick me up from school made me feel like a million bucks several times over. On other weekends I'd go to her house where there was always something going on. There were two or three young men in their early twenties who were regulars there. They weren't relatives but more like semi-permanent house guests. They were always up for shooting hoops or playing football over at the Newman's lower grass field with Gary and me, when they weren't landscaping, painting, or repairing something at the Olson's house. One afternoon, a very exotic black car pulled up in their driveway. It was a poet of some repute, there to see Mrs. Olson. She was an exceptionally good-looking woman. Interesting people of all ages seemed to be coming and going at the Olsons. My home, with just my parents, me and the cat, was dull and, well, bourgeois by comparison.

Kristin might have known I was going back to Taft in the fall, but I didn't tell her why. I saw no reason to tell her what a mess I was, the mess I was in or what I was planning on doing when I got there. Over the years I've found that if you don't pry into other people's lives, they begin to open up to you about theirs. I saw her as the kind of older sister I wish I had, and girlfriend I knew I never would have. I'm not sure what she saw in me, but at that point I didn't care.

We had one thing in common other than music. She had spent a year or two at Dana Hall, a New England all-girls prep school. With her erect posture, charm and the social graces of a debutante, she could have fit into that world if she'd wanted to. She told me her mother had been homecoming queen at Stanford and her father senior class president, but it sounded more like a confession, something to hide rather than be proud of. Given the times we were living in, I thought I could understand the why.

On the day she was going back to Colorado College after winter break, I was playing pickup football at the Newmans with Gary and the houseboys when she walked over to say goodbye. As soon as she was gone, and completely out of the blue, tears came to my eyes. I did not see that coming. And then I realized, and everyone there could see it too, how I felt about her. I think her brother Gary understood and seemed perfectly okay about it. Not wanting to come off to her parents as an underage suitor with a case of puppy love, I curbed my visits after that. If I was over at the Newman's, I'd sometimes drop by to see Gary. I liked Gary, but I was also trying to establish that I hadn't been dropping by before just to see Kristin. Mrs. Olson never mentioned Kristin during my post-Kristin visits, and I understood what that meant. Mr. and Mrs. Olson were, however, interested in Taft and whether it might be a good fit for Gary. I stopped dropping by after that. Then two things happened. Kristin started calling me from her dorm at college. And her parents invited my parents and me, along with Gary, to a formal dinner at the California Club in downtown Los Angeles to discuss Taft.

Once again, I found myself in a situation involving adults that presented nothing but bad choices. I could tell them the truth about Taft, shock everyone at the table, and leave the impression

Kristin, circa 1969

there was something seriously wrong with me. Or I could lie and come off as a "fine young man" who realized the advantages of prep school. I squirmed, hemmed and hawed throughout the dinner because I'm not a very good liar. But by the end of the evening, I came to say what both sets of parents had come to expect: Taft was a wonderful school.

Gary applied and was accepted. When I heard the news, I told myself that if he was assigned my old room in the Tower, I would do everything I could to get him out of there. But I felt like a total chump, knowing I couldn't fully protect him from a school like Taft and someone like Mr. Marx. All I could hope was that his experience would be different than mine — and that I would keep him distanced from the thing I was planning.

Meanwhile Kristin was using her roommate's credit card to call me almost every night. I was sure she would have forgotten me as soon as she was back at college. That would have been the decent thing to do. Instead, we'd spend fifteen to thirty minutes each night confessing how much we missed each other. Her hellos were breathless; her goodbyes wrenching. And yet, as miserable as those calls left me, I still floated on air every time she called. For several weeks I followed her down that long-distance rabbit hole, until the calls finally became too much. I was in over my head, and any evening she didn't call made me believe she'd come to her senses or met someone new. The last thing I needed was an achy heart. She invited me to go skiing with some of her college friends in Aspen over Easter break and we left it at that.

My parents were naturally against the idea of me going skiing with an unchaperoned bunch of college-aged students. To counter that, I invited Preston. After his parents agreed, mine caved. Life briefly returned to normal. I went to school, played guitar and listened to music. Joni Mitchell's *Ladies of the Canyon* lulled me to sleep, while albums by The Band, Taste and Free, among others, fed my dreams, inspired me to keep playing guitar and filled in many of the blanks about life that school and my parents couldn't.

My mother had started doing volunteer library work at under-funded schools in the beach town of Venice. My sisters were still in college. The Vietnam war ground on, while on the home front, protests against it and demonstrations for it escalated. And music seemed to track it all — from "For What It's Worth" to "Street Fighting Man" to "Ballad of the Green Berets." Sometimes I felt like I was sitting in the nosebleed section of the upper decks of an empty stadium watching America go down the drain, waiting until it was time for me to do what I had to do. Hoping I wouldn't end up circling the drain myself.

Except for sports, the nightly news was depressing. There seemed to be more corruption and pork-barrel politics than ever — and of course Vietnam, which was the most glaring example of how sideways things had gotten. I thought back to Taft, and how Mr. Esty and many guest speakers at vespers regularly told us we were America's future leaders. If that was true, prep schools had turned out some real lemons.

Even in laid-back Los Angeles, the future looked prickly. The spread of communism and the threat of nuclear war were rein-forced every Friday at PaliHi when the air-raid siren at the corner of El Medio and Sunset Boulevard would blare and we'd all have to take shelter under our desks. The rift between the generations was getting worse. Boys not much older than me were either going to Vietnam, applying for draft deferments, or dodging the draft altogether and leaving America for places like Canada. Those were the choices in the late 1960s for most white, upper-middle-class 18-year-old boys. Aware of the racial and social inequities that made Vietnam not a choice but an order for others added a new dimension of unfairness and hypocrisy to my small understanding of how the world worked. The system appeared corrupt and broken. As I considered my future after high school, not going to college started making more sense despite my father's repeated warning about how that would limit my options in life.

Until then, I was going to squeeze as much pleasure and adventure out of life as I could. At the start of Easter break, Preston and I flew to Colorado Springs and met up with Kristin at her dorm. We caravanned up to Aspen in several cars; Kristin accepting a ride from a guy who owned a Porsche. I was a little stung that she didn't want to ride with Preston and me so we could catch up, but I understood. The Porsche driver was handsome, and probably her new boyfriend for all I knew. I would quietly take that out on him when we got to the slopes. Meanwhile, Kristin had recently called me "Mr. Potato Head" in a letter. There was nothing I could do about that.

There were maybe nine or ten of us. Preston and I were the youngest and the social situation reminded me of Woody's "kindergarten" at ISP. We were renting a condo for the week within walking distance of Ajax Ski Mountain. Preston did not have a lot of experience but the snow was soft and the mild weather made it easy to ski. I quickly established myself as one of the better skiers in the group, which gave me the confidence to relax and hold my own with Kristin's friends in the evenings. I was having such a good time that when the week was up and everyone was getting ready to head back down, I decided to stay. There was another week before my high school classes resumed and I wanted to spend every day of it skiing. Preston decided to leave, caught a ride back to Denver and flew home on his own. I felt bad for not sticking with him, but I was having too good a time and I wasn't completely alone. Kristin and a couple of her friends had decided to stay on, too.

One of her friend's parents owned a chalet near Aspen and we stayed there the first night after our rental expired. By then the Porsche driver had tucked tail and left, leaving whatever chemistry they might have had behind, which didn't look like much to me. I skied mostly with Kristin the day after Preston left. She was a beginner-intermediate and I had to stay off the upper advanced runs if I wanted to ski with her. Which I did. By the next day, the remaining skiers in our group took a break and stayed at the chalet while Kristin and I went back to the slopes. We skied until the lifts closed, then found ourselves alone, tired and happy, at the end of another perfect day. I'd spent half the day skiing with her and the other half on the upper part of Ajax. I was happily worn out.

Carrying our skis past the parking lots to the road where we could start hitchhiking back to the chalet, we passed some construction workers exiting a condominium they were building. My feet and legs ached, it was getting cold and we were beyond tired. We paused and then stepped in through the door they'd come out of. It was warm inside. We leaned our things against the wall and listened for the sounds of more workers, but they were evidently done for the day. We sat on some buckets and stretched our legs. The idea of going back out in the cold and trudging with our equipment in the hopes of hitching a ride was dimming along with the light outside. We were sitting next to a janitor's closet that was small but big enough for us to fit inside. On a whim, for I don't know what else to call it, we decided to stay.

We might have gone out for dinner or snacked on trail-mix or candy bars. We might have gone back outdoors and found a pay phone to call her friends to tell them we weren't coming back. Either way, we spent the night together like two waifs, fully clothed but snuggled close until the first light of dawn when we had to scoot out before the workers returned. We skied again that day and went back to the condominium again that night. As I recall, we befriended the night-watchman — or possibly not — but we became brave or perhaps familiar enough to venture up to the second floor the next evening and found a condo that was finished to the point that it had a thermostat, heat and wall-to-wall carpeting. Even without furniture or drapes, it was luxury compared to the janitor's closet. We stayed there for four or five more nights.

We'd sleep on the carpet side by side with the moonlight streaming in, illuminating Ajax and turning Kristin's blond locks into a fleece of white gold. I would wake up sometimes in the middle of the night and stroke her hair while she slept. Sometimes I couldn't help wanting to do more and I would take my sweet time getting nowhere. All night long, all I could think was how beautiful she was and how lucky I was to be alive.

We flew back to LA at the end of that week. She got a cab at LAX and dropped me off half asleep at my house and then went home to hers. It was a grey, balmy day; heavy and warm, nothing like the dry, sharp air of Aspen. I felt a little hungover and lost without her. We would not have each other to depend on to survive the days and nights ahead. No more "I'll meet you back here" if we took different runs down the mountain. No more finding each other at day's end among the throngs of skiers. No more using our wits and wiles to find something to eat or shelter for the night. She was going to be home for a few more days before going back to Colorado to finish her freshman year and I was going back to finish tenth grade.

I kept all this from my parents, of course, knowing what their reaction would be. As far as they knew, it was just another ski trip and I'd made it back. That left the door open for me to visit Kristin in the time that remained. I was at her house a few nights later. I might have been invited over for dinner to tell Gary and his parents more about Taft. What I remember is sitting around the fireplace in the den later that evening when again, as if the gods were pulling strings, one by one the rest of her family drifted off, leaving us alone. I was ready to leave myself and walk home when she took my hand and led me down the hallway toward her bedroom. Sensing my unease, she told me not to worry. As we passed the door to Gary's room, she assured me that Gary would warn us in the event her mother or father came to check on us.

I looked around her room after she closed her door and disappeared into her closet. It was a girl's room all right, with stuffed animals, riding boots, perfume on the dresser along with combs and hairbrushes, all neatly set out. I was a slob by comparison and felt wrong to be there but before I had time to reconsider it, she'd reappeared in a nightgown, lit a stick of incense and walked me over to her bed.

There were two beds in her room, side by side against a wall. Each bed had white lace curtains that could be drawn to close it off from the rest of the room. Like a railroad berth and for privacy. As I stood there wondering what Joni Mitchell would do if she were in my sneakers, Kristin drew back the curtain and pulled back the covers, assuring me there was nothing to worry about.

During our nights in Aspen, although we slept next to each other, we never became lovers as the word, it now seemed to me, is usually misapplied. And while it may seem strange, it didn't matter to me if we did "it" or not. I'd simply take matters into my own hands after she'd fallen asleep, or after I started nuzzling too close and she'd tell me no. I found it a little puzzling that just two weeks after we were on our own in Aspen, she was willing to make love to me, with her parents just down the hall. But I wasn't about to grill her about that now.

I cared more about being with her at that point. We were on the same wavelength. We laughed at the same things and liked the same music. Even when we weren't talking, it felt like she could read my mind. She could snap me out of a dark mood with just a look, laugh or a word of wisdom that would sometimes make me think that maybe she saw a future together. Having never made love before (other than in my dreams) I was floating on air but worried I'd be a disappointment. We'd gotten lucky in Aspen (where I often thought the gods were making up for Taft and Mr. Marx) and managed to stay out of trouble, big and small.

Now as I looked down at her, I had a bad feeling we were taking a huge risk. I did not want to lose her but there was no way I could resist her.

She parted her gown — causing an immediate drop in value to every famous sculpture and work of art ever made. For my own insurance, I kept my jeans around my ankles, just in case someone came. I knew I was getting in way over my head. We were kissing, and they were very tender kisses along with touches that made my stomach shiver and flop. Then I heard footsteps followed by a knock on her door.

"Kristin?" It was her father.

She put her finger to her lips, slipped out of bed and drew the curtain back across to hide me. While I started wriggling my jeans back up as quietly as I could, I overheard their conversation. Her father thought he'd heard voices. Kristin assured him he was mistaken. He was not convinced. She pleaded with him but he came into her room anyway. I heard her closet door open and then the anxiety rising in her voice as he carried out his search. I heard him draw the curtain open on the other bed. At this point she was crying and begging him to go. I'd just finished pulling my pants up to my hips when he drew back the curtain on her bed. I closed my eyes, like I had with Mr. Marx, waiting for the blow I had coming.

Although he could clearly see who I was, he said nothing. After what seemed like forever, he led Kristin out of the room. I lay there for several minutes, wondering what to do in my spare time. I wanted to be with her and was ready to trade in my family for hers, and in one moment, both of those hopes seemed pretty dashed. I couldn't face him if he came back in, so I lifted the window sash next to her bed and slipped out into the night. The moon was full, or nearly so, and cast a heavenly yellow glow on the gardens outside, much as it had a few minutes before on her face and body. It was unusually pleasant out and very still. Realizing I could go anywhere in weather like that, I gave a good deal of thought to running away. Running away for good this time. I could see myself working in a coal mine next to Lee Dorsey, singing as we slipped down the shaft to start another shift. But the more I thought about it and what she must be going through, the more I knew I couldn't abandon her. She had been the only bright spot in my life over the past year. I owed her that much.

I went around to the front door and knocked. Mr. Olson answered, looking none too happy to see me. I followed him into the living room where Kristin and her mother sat crying in their robes, appearing inconsolably sad, as though they'd just discovered a mutilated deer in the backyard. They looked at me but I had no words. I suppose I was guilty of betraying her parents' trust. But that was in a universe I didn't understand. Exactly what was said I don't remember, but the gist of it was our age difference made what we were doing not just inappropriate, but mortifying. Mr. Olson told me he was about to call my parents when he'd discovered I'd fled — a rather uncalled for and unsubtle dig about my age, but I was in no position to tell him the truth, which was that I not only liked his daughter but also for some reason I was falling for her, too. I wanted to tell him I was unlucky of late and list some recent examples — but I wasn't sure a former Stanford class president would see the virtue in that or any other excuse of mine. So, I just stood there with my mouth shut and waited for the verdict. He escorted me back to Kristin's room, where I picked the rest of my felonious belongings off the floor. Then he drove me back to my parents' house. It was a quiet ride. I had hoped that because I'd come back to face the music, he might not see me in such a bad light. Might even come around to forgiving me and allow me to keep seeing her as a friend. But when he dropped me off, all he had to say was he thought it best I not see Kristin again.

I spent a sleepless night, alternating between sadness and anger. Sad for losing her and angry at her father, and adults in general, for continuing to hammer on my little existence — an existence that was looking bleaker by the minute. I thought about what my experiences at Taft had taught me: I'd learned how to survive Mr. Marx's soul crushing by breaking rules and putting up resistance. And as in any resistance, there are casualties. My battle with Taft was just around the corner. I knew it would probably cost me the future my parents envisioned, but I didn't care about that. All I cared about was that it would make me a poor candidate for a girl like Kristin and any future we might have. But I had to put that aside for now if I had any hope of salvaging my own future. Maybe someday I could explain it to her. If only I had enough time and could understand it myself. But we were out of time and out of place; and I was a long way off from understanding what was going on. By the following morning I'd made up my mind not to see her again. I'd honor my word to her father and accept the clean break he'd asked for.

She called the next day. I'd already told my parents to take a message if she did. She was obviously not attuned to the writings of Che and other revolutionaries who put the cause ahead of everything else, most of all bourgeois sentiments — because she kept calling. I avoided answering the phone and told my parents to tell her I wasn't home when she did call. She showed up at our house a day or two later. Preston and I were playing Dibble Dabble in the pool. She walked up to the edge and started breaking down, pleading with me to talk with her. I just stared up at her like she was a complete stranger. I have no idea what Preston thought. We never did talk about it. It was one of the worst moments of my life. Like watching a scene from a movie that breaks your heart in a multiple of stupid ways. She eventually got the message and walked away. That moment remains the greatest betrayal and regret of my life.

The weeks that followed passed in a blur of sadness and an attempt to get back to normal footing. I kept consoling myself that she would find another guy, not someone on a losing streak, and I would find another girl who made me feel the way she did. We were young and there had to be others out there like us. Free love was in the air after all. And if for some reason lightning didn't strike twice, there was always the fat chance that we'd meet up again someday under different circumstances, when I was older and had something going for me other than bad luck. More of which was just around the corner.

In June 1970 I turned 16 and got my learner's permit. My grandparents bought a new Buick Skylark every other year and their older ones were sometimes given or shipped out to us. It was a white convertible with red interior and mine to borrow. I didn't mind getting my license but it came loaded with adult responsibilities I didn't like – like insurance, carrying a wallet and wearing glasses, among other things. My father took me for a test drive on the Santa Monica Freeway, which was nerve-wracking and humbling. I hated being bad at something, doubly so in front of my father.

CHAPTER 18

Craig Babin was one of my oldest friends from elementary school in Santa Monica. Craig was the only son of a strained marriage. The result of his parents' passive-aggressive relationship was evident by piles of dirty dishes in the sink, fleas jumping on the shag carpet and dog hair on every surface. You could let your hair down and be a natural adolescent slob in his house without giving it a second thought, which was nice. His mother was extremely warm and welcoming though she spent most of her time on the phone. Craig was close to his father though his father was rarely there when I was around. Craig was lean and good-looking, with long, curling brown hair down to his shoulders. Girls were interested in him and he returned the favor, although his insecurities, like mine, made him a hard nut for any one girl to crack. But he was so open, smart, warm and funny that everyone either liked , or in the case of girls, adored him. The hardest I've ever laughed was with him. We decided to take a camping trip in late July to Kings Canyon National Park. It was in the same area where I had gone to Bob Mathias Sierra Boys Camp. Craig's father was not entirely on board with the plan. He thought we were too young and inexperienced for the four-hour drive but finally gave in. We left early on the morning of July 28. We were in the Skylark and I was behind the wheel. About fifty miles north of Los Angeles, we got a flat tire. I pulled over to the shoulder of the freeway with cars whizzing by and we somehow managed to change the tire. That gave us a dose of confidence and off we went.

The turnoff to Kings Canyon is near Visalia. We left the flat farmland of the San Joaquin Valley and started climbing up the Sierra foothills. When we passed a general store called Snowline, I knew we were close to the turnoff to the Mathias Camp. The two-lane road we were on had lots of sharp curves and very few guardrails. We were several thousand feet above the valley floor. I finally saw the mailbox for the camp and the dirt road that led into it on my left. It was nearly noon and we didn't have much farther to go — maybe another ten miles or so until the park entrance. I wanted to show Craig where I'd gone to summer camp and so we turned left and took the road in.

The camp looked much the same: log cabin bunkhouses spread among golden hills and the main lodge where we ate and watched Bob Mathias movies. We drove up to the main lodge and parked. It was lunchtime and campers and counselors were all heading in. I recognized one of the counselors and he invited us to stay for lunch. Afterward he got up and asked me to reminisce about camp in front of the hundred or so campers and counselors. Public speaking petrified me and after saying a few inane things about how wonderful the camp looked, we left quickly.

My nerves were jangled and I wanted a cigarette to calm down. We took a right when we got back to the main road and headed back down to the Snowline general store where we bought a pack of Winstons. It was sunny and warm. We had the convertible top down as we drove back up the road to the park entrance. We'd been listening to the radio most of the way up and a song came on by Mungo Jerry about summertime and "having women on our mind." We cranked it up and as I finished my cigarette, for some reason I handed it to Craig to put out in the ashtray. It seemed a bit out of reach to me. The handoff did not go well and the cigarette dropped in his lap. I'd had my eyes on the road until then but I glanced over to see if he'd recovered it.

In that instant, everything turned green and I no longer felt the tires on the road. The car landed with a thud. Bouncing down a steep grade, it rapidly gained speed. My eyes jitterbugged and my life did indeed flash before my eyes. A tree appeared dead ahead and the Buick slammed into it in what seemed like slow motion. I got out of the car and started climbing up the slope on my hands and knees when a hand grabbed mine. It turned out that the driver behind us came around the curve I'd missed and saw the cloud of dust. When I got up to the road, Craig was already there, covered in blood. The windshield on his side had imploded and showered him with glass. The man who'd been following us turned out to be a doctor. He treated Craig while we waited for the ambulance.

We were taken to a hospital in Fresno where Craig received forty stitches. I had no injuries except a fat lip caused by the steering wheel. My father flew up and the three of us flew back to LA later that evening. Craig looked like a mummy with blood seeping through his bandages. People stared at us as we walked through the airport. My father and I drove back up a few weeks later to visit the crash site and settle with the wrecking company.

Where I'd driven off the road, there were places on either side that were sheer drop-offs, hundreds of feet down. The path the Buick took was still a visible scar. The car was headed in a straight line toward a large dead branch that would have impaled us, followed by a sheer drop just beyond it that would have finished us off. But just before that, the tire tracks veered left, ending at the foot of a deeply gouged sapling pine that saved our lives. For whatever reason the car had suddenly veered left. I knew it had nothing to do with my driving skills.

I proved that again on the drive back. After we made it down to flat land, my father let me take the wheel to get my confidence back. We were coming to a four-way intersection somewhere near Tulare when my father told me to slow down. I ended up skidding halfway through the intersection. Fortunately, no cars were coming the other way. My father's cross-eyed look made up for that bit of good luck.

I was in a blue funk after that. I'd nearly killed one of my best friends and ruined what promised to be a great camping trip. I'd go over to visit Craig and we'd play board games and cards while he was recovering, but the reception from his parents was neutral and understandably so. He was their only child and my carelessness had nearly killed him. Craig was more forgiving but there were no more discussions about camping adventures.

My parents were supportive and urged me to put the accident behind me. Meanwhile I transitioned from suspecting I might be a serial failure to proving it. All I wanted to do was stay in my room, play guitar, listen to records and lick my wounds. My emotional recovery from the accident and its aftermath continued on and off through August. There were some parties and beach days that helped and then before I knew it, my leave was up. It was time to report back to Taft.

PART 7

Something in the Air

Bruce and I were in a triple on the third floor of the CPT wing. Our other roommate was Taylor Rockwell. "Tay" had been in our lower mid class. He was not part of our old lower mid stairwell crew so I didn't really know him. He was tall and thin with long, straggly auburn hair. He came from a well-to-do family that lived near Chicago. Bruce and I would occasionally make fun of his earnest attempts at being a hipster, but he was a genial guy. He tried hard to make us like him and was easy to get along with. His taste in music leaned toward *Jesus Christ Superstar* and he rather looked the part. He joined Taft's Masque and Dagger Society, the school drama club, and set his earthly sights on a cute, older girl I remembered from my old Middlebury days. She was a member of the all-girls theater troupe at St. Margaret's and regularly appeared in Taft plays that required females. Her reputation around Taft was fast and loose. Watching our Jesus-looking roommate try to charm his way into her pants provided us with some good chuckles that fall. Otherwise, chuckles were in short supply.

Bruce never brought up Mr. Marx's rumor about me. And I did not tell him it was my only reason for coming back. My plan was quite simple. Like I did when I first moved to LA when I was 8, I was going to have to alter my personality to deal with the situation. Somehow, I had to prove that the rumor about me couldn't be true. I would have to become such a defiant thorn in Taft's backside that everyone there would remember me for that. I'd erase any memories of me as a weak lower mid with new radical ones. I thought it was a good plan. But I had to string it out long enough to let it sink in to everyone's conscience. I couldn't do something stupid that would get me kicked out right away. And of course, I couldn't let anyone know what I was up to.

I merely told Bruce, and anyone else who asked, that living at home was worse than Taft. Most had no trouble believing me as many felt the same. As bad as Taft was, we were at least out from under our parents' microscope. And we had each other's back for moral support.

My long-term plan was to eventually escape somewhere where the air was clean and expectations were low. Perhaps Norway, where girls like Kristin were surely as plentiful as reindeer. Whenever my parents asked me what I wanted to do and I'd tell them some vague dream of mine like that, they'd crush it. To them, that was tantamount to throwing my life away. I'd tell them I wasn't running away from life. I was running *to* a better future they just didn't happen to like. Taft didn't seem to care what I wanted to be. No master, administrator or Mr. Esty ever asked me why I returned. I appeared to be of no special interest to any adult there, with the possible exception of Mr. Marx, whom I hadn't run into yet.

Bob Golfman was in Bruce's room one evening. They were in the middle of discussing something that sounded heavy and private. I decided to make myself scarce. Before I did, they asked if I remembered Bill Waldron. I thought back to my image of Bill as a lower mid in Mr. Wynne's history class. How in his Taft blazer, tie and slacks he looked perfectly at ease in prep school and that a perfect four years would play out, followed by another perfect four years at an Ivy League college and then a wonderful marriage to an equally attractive and intelligent partner who'd gone to all the right schools herself. I didn't trust anyone who fit the mold as perfectly as he did. But I also remembered him as a hard person not to like. I'd forgotten all about the newspaper article.

Bruce and Bob then told me how Bill's fairy tale didn't pan out. This was close to the anniversary of his death; around the time my grandparents had sent me the newspaper article. Bill was a

I am in the front row, second from left, with Bob Golfman and Bruce Maclean, in the middle of the center row, Taft School. 1970-71

stagehand in the Masque and Dagger Society, along with Bruce
and Bob. They were striking the last set after the first school play
of the year. Bob was talking to Bill with his back turned. When
Bill didn't respond, Bob turned around and, like a little bit of
stage magic, Bill had disappeared. Golfman looked down through
the trap door that was used to move large sets to and from the
basement. Bill lay motionless on the concrete floor below. No
one saw what happened. Speculation was he'd touched a hot
stage light and fell backward. Bill lived on life support for a day
and a half before his parents pulled the plug.

I was not particularly surprised. I already knew that if you were
in the wrong place at the wrong time, Taft was a dangerous
place. By then I'd developed a habit of inserting myself in other
people's misfortunes. How I reacted to this was the same as when
I first read about it in the clipping the year before: if it had been
me instead of Waldron, it would have served my parents right.

Always the optimist despite the facts, I decided to give my football career one last try. I'd grown since my lower mid-year. I was
taller, my upper body more developed and my shoulders broader.
My legs and ankles were still reed thin, however, and my thighs
and waist were probably more suited for girls' field hockey. Still,
I showed up for the varsity tryouts hoping to make the team and
play for the legendary Mr. Stone.

More than Dean Oscarson or any master at Taft, Larry Stone was
someone no student wanted to get on the wrong side of. He was
a double barrel-chested, tough-looking hombre who would pass
masters, non-athletes and anyone other than a varsity football or
baseball player in the main hallway with a general expression of

disapproval. That look would change to outright contempt for any student with long hair or who looked physically weak. But his obsession to field winning teams, even though they perennially played second fiddle to Lance Odden's varsity hockey teams, appealed to me. I thought we were both outliers in that sense, and I was hoping my speed, height and soft hands might make me a wide receiver that he could count on.

I went out for the wide receiver position but did not impress Mr. Stone or his assistants with my "pop and ginger." When the final positions and depth charts were posted, I was third-string tight end. The two boys ahead of me, Brian Lacy and someone I can't remember, were far bigger and stronger and I knew I would never get the chance to play. I decided to try out for JV soccer instead, but first I had to tell Mr. Stone. That would be like telling General Patton I wanted to transfer to the British army and serve high tea to Monty. When I finally summoned the courage and found a private moment, I told him I was quitting because I didn't get the position I went out for. Mr. Stone called me a *quittah* and gave me a patented reaming for wasting his time.

Mr. Cobb was the JV soccer coach and altogether different from Mr. Stone. Cobb was a chain smoker with thin black hair, sunken cheeks and a rather fatalistic expression and attitude. He had gallows humor and preferred to let us scrimmage so he could finish his cigarettes in peace rather than teaching new skills. He was the only high school coach I had who understood that having fun playing sports was not a cancer. When the preseason was over and we started league play, he liked to win as much as we did but he took the wins and losses in stride. He let us work things out for ourselves and we became a better and more cohesive team for it. There was only one game he was serious about, and that would come at the end of the season when we played archrival Hotchkiss. He did not want to lose that game.

On junior varsity soccer team in 1970. John Hagelin is in lower right, Derric Parmenter in upper right.

I was walking off the practice field on the late warm afternoon of September 18 when someone told me Jimi Hendrix had died. A few weeks later Janis Joplin was dead too. Their deaths were big news on campus. When the causes came to light (alcohol-related asphyxiation and heroin overdose, respectively) it validated the argument that if the Woodstock generation was wrong about recreational drugs, we might be wrong about everything else.

My room was in the same main building cluster as before but far removed from the HDT wing and Mr. Marx. I presumed he still resided in the Tower. Eventually I knew the day would come when our paths would cross. That was a moment I'd worried about ever since I made the decision to come back. What would he make of my return? Did he know I'd heard about the rumor he'd spread? Would he suspect I was back for vengeance? Or would he think I'd overcome my lower-mid prudishness and decided I wanted to rekindle our "relationship?" Would he say nothing, or try to ruin my reputation again? There was no telling.

Dick Cobb, my JV soccer coach in 1970/71

He must have known I was coming back because he did not seem surprised to see me in the main hall outside his classroom one morning. He looked the same as I remembered: from the hand-me-down sport coat to the wispy hair and thick-framed glasses and lecher's grin. Like an estranged couple who know each other's secrets, we eyeballed each other in an attempt to see where things stood. I glowered the most contemptible look I could muster. He looked at me with a mocking grin that said I was back on his turf now and whatever game I was playing, his hand would always be stronger than mine. And that was possibly the last time I saw him.

Down in the trenches of student life, Taft had not changed much in the year I was away. One notable difference was that the BFD movement had fizzled out after the '69 senior class graduated. This left a void for how students coped with the pressures of school. There were several new faces in my upper mid class — not that our class had become bigger; the new faces were replacements for students who had either left voluntarily or been dismissed. Our class pecking order had not changed. Erik Kitchen and Bruce Braine were still atop the class academically. Peter Miller and John Taft remained our class leaders for their athletic achievements (football for Peter and soccer for John) and outgoing personalities. John and Peter were often chosen by Mr. Cunningham to show prospective new students and parents around the school.

I noticed a subtle change in my old friend from San Francisco, John Dant. It wasn't that he had changed so much as that the Haight-Ashbury counterculture hippie vibe that he alone came in with as a lower mid had begun to catch on with the rest of the student body. In the 1968 Taft yearbook, no senior holds a musical instrument. In 1971, over seven percent of the seniors hold one in their senior photo — mostly guitars. Rock and roll was like an invasive species that was starting to choke out the old phylum and order that had been carefully cultivated at Taft for over a century. John Dant was a counterculture loner when he arrived at Taft as a lower mid. Some in the administration would have pegged him as a potential problem. Two years later, John would prove far more prescient about the future than they were. I suspect a student leadership role was on the table if John wanted it. They had no choice really. If they could entice John to become head monitor his senior year, they knew he had the respect of the students, and that could be pivotal in helping them maintain control.

John's transformation at Taft began with another John — John Small — Taft's cross-country coach. Mr. Small's Nietzschean

John Dant, second from left. Coach John Small, fourth from left with sweatband and white t-shirt.

outlook meshed with John's Zen-like personality. John went out for cross country and Mr. Small became his adviser — an example of a successful master-student relationship, unlike mine. Mr. Small's stature at Taft was mythical. He was older than Mr. Marx, but they shared some traits. They were both bachelors, had their own apartments at school, and did not socialize with other teachers. Mr. Small taught German — perhaps not with the same zeal that Mr. Marx taught Latin and Greek. But he probably didn't need to belittle students to earn their respect either. He could also have snapped Mr. Marx in two, but that's probably beside the point. Mr. Small had a physique that made you wonder if he lifted weights in his sleep. He inspired performances from his runners that went beyond their natural abilities. In a photograph in the 1971 annual, one of his athletes is blowing chunks mid-stride.

Cross country was not a big sport at Taft. "Ringers" were not recruited and given scholarships like in football and hockey. Mr. Small had to build his teams from the ground up. I don't think Mr. Esty and Mr. Small were close. I base that on the observation that Mr. Small had the wizened face of a German field general, constantly overcoming stupid tactical decisions by his desk-bound superior.

John Dant would not break any cross-country records at Taft, but the following year he would be elected head monitor. In Coach Small, John found a master he could trust and bond with. In Mr. Esty, John had a headmaster who needed all the help he could get to bridge the widening gap between the students and his administration.

For parents who could afford the tuition, some saw Taft as an opportunity to park their sons somewhere safe with a guaranteed return on their investment while America sorted out its problems — or they sorted out their own. Mine were on that spectrum and so I gravitated to boys like that — boys like me. There was a growing number of "lost boys" for whom the goal of getting into an Ivy League school was starting to look rigged in their favor rather than idealistic. Spiro Agnew, Nixon's vice president at the time, labeled our generation's malcontents "an effete corps of impudent snobs." Meanwhile, our parents were determined to keep us on the straight and narrow path to nowhere. Take your pick. Either way, we were being bent, folded, spindled and mutilated, with very little say in the matter.

Had the school's administration or the masters been aware of how America's changing culture was affecting us, that might have led to more open dialogue in the classroom and things might have turned out differently. As it was, their agenda and tactics had not changed with the times. They were full steam ahead with their college admissions goals and in lockstep with our parents who were footing the bill. In some ways I couldn't have asked for a better environment to carry on with my plan.

I thought about killing Mr. Marx though not because I hated him. I found him impossible to hate. He was like a rabid dog. Putting him down and out of his misery seemed like a humane thing to do, and good for the safety of others. More to the point, it would send a message to the administration that we weren't going to put up with masters like him put in unchecked control over us. Mulling over how to kill him and get away with it became a pleasant diversion in the early weeks of my return.

How to kill a master briefly became a serious topic of discussion during our late-night bull sessions. The main stairways in HDT and CPT had narrow, rectangular slots when viewed from the top of the stairs down to the basement. A Ben Franklin half-dollar coin falling from the top floor could probably crack the Liberty Bell. What might happen to a master buttonholed by a student in the basement if that coin was "accidently" kicked off a ledge by another student five stories up? I drifted off to sleep several times with that fantasy playing in my head. That plan was never put into action but others were already in motion.

My approach to undermine Taft began immediately. I'd brought a skateboard with me and set up slalom courses on the sloped driveway in front of Congdon House. This drew the attention of several masters and students, most of whom watched with curiosity laced with suspicion. There was one other student from the West Coast who knew how to skateboard, Derric Parmenter, a soccer teammate. This was the introduction of skateboarding at Taft. We'd sidewalk surf outside when the weather was nice and down in the basement corridors when it wasn't. The sour looks on masters' faces as we blew past them and weaved around students was priceless. It relegated to a bygone era the weekend tradition of launching toy sailboats on the Pond under the gaze of a nostalgic master.

My first class was held in a tiered lecture hall in the science building with about a hundred upper mids and seniors. It was physics taught by Mr. North, a large, garrulous man with a booming voice. Like Mr. Reiff, he was passionate but unlike my experience in lower mid biology, I was quickly snowed under by the subject matter. It did not help that he delivered his lectures with the speed of a particle accelerator. I understood the difference between velocity and acceleration but had no aptitude or interest for the multitude of equations involving those concepts.

Mr. North used a slide projector to shine equations on the screen behind him. I was not shy about raising my hand to ask questions. I truly wanted to understand what he was teaching. My parents were paying for it after all and I wanted them to get their money's worth. But after a while I could tell he was becoming exasperated with me. Other students began to groan every time my hand went up. I finally stopped interrupting.

For a while I remained after class, asking questions to try to catch up. It was no use. I just didn't have aptitude for physics and all the equations and math that went with it. There was an air table that Mr. North used to demonstrate the movement of objects in a frictionless state and my only enjoyment in his classroom came down to playing air hockey on it before and after class. At some point, after learning about angstrom units, wave lengths and amplitudes ad nauseum, I asked him how we would apply those things to the real world — outside of rockets and parabolic trajectories into outer space. He smiled and told me nodal lines were used in solder baths. That seemed fitting. Thanks to physics, my GPA was taking a bath of its own.

Math in the afternoon was held in a smaller classroom with maybe fifteen students taught by Mr. Philpit, a first-year teacher who looked fresh out of college. Pudgy, shy, with a distinct lisp, he did his darnedest to establish order by issuing slide rules and introducing us to sines and cosines on the first day. At the end of the first week, I raised my hand and asked for an example of how we might apply what he was teaching to life. He was perplexed and looked around to the other students for help. But when they all remained silent, waiting for an answer because they were curious, too, he grew flustered. My question became a running joke in his class. Other students picked up on it and would ask him the same thing whenever we needed a laugh or a break from the monotony. But because he was sweet and good-natured, we let him remain in control.

I had Spanish with Mr. Wayne Yankus. He was trim, mid-thirties and had the air of a young man in his prime. He was one of the few married teachers at Taft, which probably explained his perpetual good humor and bright smile. His wife was a vivacious Hispanic brunette and they appeared to be a very happy couple. Another rarity at Taft. All around his classroom were colorful posters of sun-drenched Mexico and Spain, along with *serapes* and other knick-knacks they'd collected during their summer travels and sabbaticals. I could not play the same card with Mr. Yankus that I did with Mr. Philpit. He was too hip for those tricks. I had little interest in learning Spanish. I'd visited Mexico City over Christmas 1964 with my mother's side of the family. My older cousins took me to a packed, sweltering movie theater one night to watch *The Great Escape*," where my bowels fittingly had a great escape of their own. Three long hours later and back at the hotel, my mother carefully pried a perfectly molded replica of my rump out of my tighty-whities. It was hard as an adobe brick. The last thing the good citizens of Mexico needed was another visit from me.

As I look back in my yearbook, I think I had Oliver Everett for history. He was one of several new, young masters. I don't remember what he taught because none of it explained what was going on in the era we were living in. It wasn't all boring or useless. Even I could appreciate how ancient history has some bearing on modern history. But at the pace Taft was teaching history, we'd all be a hundred years old by the time we got to the Middle Ages.

At any rate, I did not return to Taft to learn new things. I was there to prove I was a bad boy and my modus operandi in class was to cause disruption. I did that by regularly questioning what we were learning. If we were being "prepped," for life after Taft, why weren't we learning things that were relevant to the world around us? I took a great deal of satisfaction in sowing those seeds of doubt, and after a while I think many of my classmates came around to thinking there was validity to my questions.

Several new masters like Mr. Philpit were in their first teaching jobs. They knew their subject matter well but their inexperience showed. Whatever idealism or novel approach to teaching they may have arrived with, most were quick to adapt to Taft's relentless study workload as the tried-and-true way of keeping students occupied and in line.

There was something new and popular at Taft that was absent my lower mid year. It was called the "circle game." Someone would make a circle with their thumb and forefinger and if someone else looked and you pulled it away before they broke your circle, you got to punch them in the shoulder. Vice versa if someone broke it before you pulled it away. All provided you brushed off their shoulder after the punch. If not, they got to punch *you* back.

Some of the masters would even engage in it. It was the kind of game prisoners might play to keep from going insane.

Another new, young master on the scene was Robert Rozelle, my English teacher. He wore a vest, sported a mustache and looked like a hotshot college professor. He was compact of build and good-looking. He gave off the aura that he was pretty hip guy who was on "our" side as it were. As he introduced himself, I could tell that other students were already looking up to him and were willing to bond. He was exactly the kind of teacher Taft needed, and therefore a problem for me. If I was going to undermine him, I needed to cast doubt about him. So, I conjured him up as someone I could easily resent, and tried to get the rest of the class to see him that way too: A smug, self-assured teacher — expecting to woo a class of pretty coeds in their freshman year of college — hiding his disappointment as he looks out at a room full of pimply-faced horndogs.

While he was laying out his curriculum for the fall semester, I decided to test him. I got out of my chair, walked to the back of the room and sat on the floor. He paused, thought about what to do as the whole class knew I'd just challenged him, and then lost his nerve (or more likely, kept his cool) and went on outlining his agenda for the semester as though nothing had happened. I took my regular seat after a week of sitting on the floor, but I'd scored a big victory and the damage was done. In my ragged logic, I'd made up my mind that I would take out my revenge on Mr. Rozelle for what Taft had done to me. When I found out he was one of the floor masters in CPT, just down the hall from our room, it made my task that much easier. I could take aim at him both day and night.

Mr. Esty, Mr. Holroyd (the new chaplain who replaced Mr. Zaeder) and occasionally Mr. Odden continued spouting the same platitudes at vespers. We were the *noblesse oblige*, the future leaders and shapers of America. This was their firm, polite way of reminding us that the antiwar protests, sit-ins and adminis- tration building takeovers raging on college campuses all over America would not be tolerated at Taft.

We were also reminded to stay away from drugs, at least until we were out of Taft. It was one of Mr. Esty's favorite vespers topics. His suggestion to get "naturally high" was about the only sage piece of advice I ever heard from him. Long on warnings and statistics about drugs, his speeches were short on details of how to achieve "a natural high" in a place with so many unnatural lows.

I had three reasons for not doing drugs at Taft: I wanted to remain clear-headed in my mission to disrupt, I wanted others to rise up with me and not zone out, and I didn't want to hand Taft a gift of a reason to kick me out. Bruce was the opposite of me regarding drugs, and yet we remained fast friends and roommates. We still shared a prisoner's fondness for cigarettes and although we were now allowed to smoke up at the Wade, we continued lighting up in the stairwells after lights out. For old time's sake.

Bruce still had the same physical appearance and personality he had as a lower mid, but he'd grown more cynical. His way of surviving Taft was to treat it as a goof, and he'd often revert to a childlike persona, saying things like "funny boy — you laugh" to deflect whatever good-natured insult I might toss his way. In actual fact he was a very bright and capable student. Had Taft's curriculum been relevant, he probably could and would have sailed right through. But like me, he was more interested in what was going on outside Taft's walls than in. I got a subscription to *Rolling Stone* magazine and he subscribed to *Time*, and between those two magazines we were able to keep up with music and current events. I eventually sent *Rolling Stone* founder Jann Wenner a note, announcing my cancellation after one of his critics dismissed Paul Kossoff's guitar playing with Free as mediocre. For good measure I added that his magazine wasn't paying enough attention to Rory Gallagher and Taste. I'm sure Mr. Wenner never got over it. Which to this day makes two of us.

Cat Steven's *Tea for the Tillerman* was regularly heard on our floor, as were some of the other mellow, introspective songwriters like Elton John, James Taylor and Carole King. They were a balm to the more sensitive adolescent parts of our brains, and a counterbalance to the edgier, angrier and more sexually charged music of the Stones, Doors, Jefferson Airplane, Led Zeppelin, Santana and new bands like Alice Cooper and the MC5.

I learned how to play "One Sunny Day" by Fleetwood Mac (when they still called themselves Peter Green's Fleetwood Mac). I would walk up and down the hallway some nights playing my Orpheus guitar and singing at the top of my lungs to try to get a party started. Bob Golfman and Bruce would sometimes join in while most other students closed their doors.

When it came to recreational drugs, Bruce was part LSD pioneer Owsley Stanley and part New York cop Frank Serpico. Its use never altered his core personality. Drugs mostly just made him happy. He'd giggle and say things like "your face is melting" when he was high, or laugh with childlike wonder at what he was seeing. He would time a tab of mescaline or psilocybin in order to start tripping in a particular class. When Bruce found out that another student was planning to bring in speed (or perhaps heroin), he put his foot down. To Bruce, there were good drugs that opened your mind and there were bad drugs, like speed and heroin, that could close it for good. Bruce threatened to turn in the would-be dealer and that ended it. As much as drugs were outside my interest, I was actually quite proud of him for that. More than anyone else at Taft and far more than Mr. Esty — whose "natural high" campaign was an Alice in Wonderland bit of wishful thinking — Bruce had his finger on the pulse and a fair amount of control over what drugs entered Taft. Bruce and I did experiment with one edible — a strict macrobiotic brown rice diet that we'd read somewhere would produce an epic high. It produced epic hunger instead.

The most interesting and telling moments at Taft all occurred outside the classroom. We had a stereo in our room and late one October afternoon, approaching twilight time, I put on the second Free album and we fell under its spell, staring out the window as the sky changed from blue to orange to pink until the needle lifted from the last song on side two. We were naturally high after listening to Paul Rogers remind us of all the things in life we were missing out on.

On another afternoon, we were in our room with the window open when we heard a loud crack on a playing field down below. It sounded like a gunshot only it wasn't. It was Tom Burley's leg getting snapped by another player who missed the soccer ball and kicked his shin instead.

There was an upper mid who came into our room one afternoon and brazenly put the moves on Bruce. We laughed it off but kept our distance from him the rest of the year. There were a lot of bright and gifted students at Taft who, for one reason or another, delved into cults or behavior that bordered on the bizarre. One time just before mandatory lights out, we were getting ready to call it a night. Our window was open and we heard a commotion outside. It was an odd sound, being that we were three stories up with nothing but a concrete pad far below us. We looked over and saw a pair of legs swinging in and out of our window. They belonged to John Hagelin, the boy whose tailbone was nearly impaled by the water pipe during our tray sliding nights lower mid year. After letting go of the gutter he was swinging from, he flew halfway into our room and stuck another landing. He just smiled and walked out without a word.

While Erik Kitchen and Bruce Braine were still neck and neck academically, John Hagelin continued skating by on sheer brilliance. Both John and his roommate, Derek Niederman, could have taught the most advanced math and physics courses had they not been more inclined to spice up their lives. Doing the unthinkable until they made it look mundane. In one of their more infamous adventures, they allegedly hot-wired the school ambulance one night, drove it two hours to Derek's parents' house to raid the liquor cabinet, and made it back before dawn —hungover but otherwise uncaught and unscathed.

The slate roofs of the main cluster of buildings at Taft were, generally speaking, deadly steep. Like the one above our room that Hagelin slid down to perform his trapeze act. But there were other areas with hips, valleys and flat spots that were relatively safe to walk on. After discovering the access hatch to the roof, Hagelin mapped out several evening roof strolls for the less adventurous, including one with an unexpected clear view into Mr. Van Sickle's apartment.

Mr. Van Sickle was head of the music department. His most pronounced feature was his full, sensual lips. His second most pronounced feature was his wife. They made an interesting couple. She was coy and demure in the dining room, rarely making eye contact with anyone other than her husband. She was also several inches taller than Mr. Van Sickle and seemed to be shyly aware she was arguably the best-looking wife on campus. I could imagine Mr. Van Sickle plucking her out of obscurity while on a piano tour in some eastern European country before he settled down and took the job at Taft. During one of our evening strolls, we caught sight of her through their window, taking off her dress, revealing the white slip she wore underneath and a little more insight into the contours of her body. Interest in the evening walks picked up after that. My memory of this is not the greatest for we all knew what we were doing was wrong. But our desire to see a female body in its full glory outvoted our collective conscience. We all wanted to see her for the same reason a starving person craves a morsel of food and will do almost anything for it. In the confines of an all-male environment, our brief sojourns as Peeping Toms became just one more slippery slope from wanting to be normal to sliding into a world of abnormality.

CHAPTER 20

Our big JV soccer game with Hotchkiss finally arrived at our field on a cool, overcast afternoon. Mr. Cobb, looking grimmer than usual, was smoking two cigarettes at the same time as we warmed up on the sidelines. We had a decent record, but Hotchkiss was either undefeated or close to it. During Mr. Cobb's pep talk before the game, he reminded us how much this game meant to him; something we already knew and were well prepared for despite the odds against us. We had several talented players and we'd become a loose bunch that enjoyed scrimmaging and playing pranks on each other. I had no soccer skills when I went out for the team, so soccer started out as a bit of a lark for me, but as the season progressed, I wanted to get better and play well for him. Even though he was a master, and therefore my enemy of sorts, he was different — someone who didn't teach down to us and who knew when to turn us loose and let us play. But to let us know just how serious he was about winning that afternoon; he upped the ante by promising to take the best offensive and defensive players of the game out to dinner.

My position was right fullback, the last line of defense before our goal, and my job was to neutralize the Hotchkiss attack in general and their right winger in particular. With visions of a juicy steak, I went out and played like a crazed sodbuster protecting my little homestead — harassing, shoving, kicking and, just shy of biting — heading or kicking the ball back up field whenever their winger dared enter my turf. I believe our standout captain Peter White scored the winning goal — or one of them anyway — and was voted the offensive player of the game. No surprise there. When it came to the best defensive player, Mr. Cobb strung it out by praising the collective effort on defense, but the one effort that stood out to him the most was mine.

I don't remember much about the dinner. Mr. Cobb was his usual deadpan self and said little except how much it meant for him to beat Hotchkiss. He took it personally, offered a reward with no strings attached, and always treated his players with respect and without a subservient attitude. He would go on to become one of Taft's longest serving masters. He was a bachelor as far as I know. Perhaps the only one I would have trusted to be around alone. He died a few years ago, and as the *Taft Bulletin* reminded all who would follow in his path, so great was his love for Taft that he left his estate to the school.

Bruce and Woody had remained in touch. Woody was a sophomore at Harvard and Bruce and I decided to visit him over Thanksgiving break. By then, forging a permission slip to escape for a weekend was so simple it defied belief. My parents would have been shocked if they knew what I was getting away with. Which was another reason I preferred Taft to home. The two of us walked through Watertown then started hitchhiking up to Cambridge. We found our way to Woody's place — Dunster Hall.

Dunster reminded me of ISP, old and venerable, with rickety wooden staircases, creaky floors and stained carpets. Loud music blasted from seemingly every room as we made our way upstairs. Woody opened the door with a cigarette dangling from his lips and welcomed us to his new digs which looked the same as his old digs at Taft, only bigger. The living room was filled with old sofas and chairs, stained with spilled wine and cigarette burns. There was the sweet smell of tobacco and something else I couldn't put my finger on until one of his flatmates opened a baggie and filled a large waterpipe on the coffee table. We gathered around and took turns at the hummingbird feeder. People drifted in and out as we reminisced with Woody about the bad old days at Taft and our harrowing trips to ISP. Woody had clearly moved on from Taft. For me and Bruce, school was back in session.

There were parties almost every weekend and, as coeds occupied every other floor, the parties were that much better. Some of Woody's friends dismissed us as teeny-boppers, but we didn't care. We quickly learned how to act around them: when to stay out of the way, when to be quiet, when to speak up and when to get lost. Cambridge was a much better town to be footloose in than New York. Bruce and I wandered down one of the back alleys and found a little sub shop called Tommy's that made juicy thin-sliced roast beef grinders so thick we could hardly get our mouths around them. In the evenings before heading back to Woody's to sleep on the floor or couch, we'd wander around the Green, which resembled a traveling circus show — from hustlers hawking jewelry out of their trench coats to the Vietnam vet in green fatigues telling us to fork over the money for a lid of pot "*most rikki-tick*." Bordering the Green were bustling pawn, jewelry, tobacco shops and music stores. I bought an album hand-stamped *Red Ball* that was purportedly a Rolling Stones bootleg of a live concert recorded on a smuggled tape player. It was practically unintelligible and even more unlistenable but it was definitely the Stones and still worth every penny.

Hitchhiking back and forth from Watertown to Cambridge was half the fun and adventure. It had the same twin elements of danger and surprise as our midnight rambles to and from ISP. People who picked us up tended to be risk takers or in need of some human contact to alleviate their long, lonely drive. Some would confide in us to get their secrets out. Some were so manically joyful that you knew they were a little off. Most were normal and kind, just helping a couple of boys get to where they were going. All of them taught us something about their lives, and life outside of school.

Two teenage boys with their thumbs out don't naturally draw the same attention as Claudette Colbert did in *It Happened One Night*, so there was a lot of standing around by the side of the road. We were having bad luck catching a ride one evening and it got to be very late — too late to make it to Cambridge without disturbing Woody in the middle of the night. We were getting ready to quit and thumb it back to Taft when a car slowed and pulled over on the shoulder. There were two girls inside, older than us, but not out of the question older. We got in the back seat and told them where we were headed. They were good looking and looked like they were looking for a good time. They were quite interested in us, where we were going, and why. Bruce and I read each other's mind, knowing if we were going to get anywhere, we would have to leave prep school out of the equation. We acted like we weren't expecting any special favors but that it was getting to be late — too late to make it to Cambridge without waking up the band; a fact of life we were used to. We claimed we were roadies for a rock and roll outfit. "Which one?" We picked one we knew they'd never heard of: It could have been May Blitz or Uriah Heep.

I don't think they bought our story, but they didn't seem to care. I don't think they told us what they did. They could have been flight attendants, nurses or factory girls. They just seemed to be out looking for a little adventure and Bruce and I happened to be in the right place at the right time. We stuck to our story even when they tried to poke some good-natured holes in it, suggesting we looked a little young to be roadies. But they were in too light a mood to let facts ruin a good story, and as we neared their exit, either out of mercy, curiosity or both, they offered to let us spend the night at their place. They made us scrambled eggs and toast and then invited each of us to sleep in their separate bedrooms.

As though I was used to situations like this, I casually stripped down to my boxer shorts, made a pillow out of my clothes and hunkered down on the rug under a blanket she'd given me. She climbed into bed and said goodnight. I said goodnight back in a way that I thought would pass for a road warrior: low and weary. I decided she would have to make the first move. She'd been beyond nice and trusting and now it was my turn to return the favor and remain cool. And I stuck hard by that decision, made easier by the fact that I could think of nothing else to say, until the soft rhythm of her breathing let me know she'd fallen asleep.

I don't know if Bruce stuck to his roadie impersonation or not. We didn't talk about it when we were back out on the road the following morning. All I know is I spent a sleepless night on the floor with heaven five feet away, wishing I were older and not who I was.

It was during winter term that I made most of my trips up to Cambridge to stay at Woody's. A couple of times after an away JV basketball game, I'd watch the rest of the team board the bus for the trip back to Taft and then make my way down a two-lane country blacktop to find a good hitchhiking spot. It was often a long wait between cars. To learn something useful, I taught myself how to juggle with rocks.

I knew why I liked going up to see Woody and hang out in Cambridge. It was part of my education and a great way to escape the doldrums of another weekend at Taft. I still wasn't sure what Woody got out of it. One trait Bruce and I shared was an aversion to growing up, and there were times we'd say or do something really immature and embarrass Woody in front of his friends or piss him off in private. We would know it immediately and hang our heads, and then he'd impart a little Woody wisdom and leave it at that.

That Bruce and I could drop by any weekend and crash at his place was a testament to Woody's stature at Dunster — much like it was at Taft. We took part in the bull sessions and wormed our way into his parties. Woody never discussed his personal life with us. Aside from his pro-Arab views, anti-bourgeois sentiments and command of French, he was all about having a good time; enjoying life filled with lively, leisurely conversation.

"Meanwhile back at the oasis, the Arabs were eating their dates," was a line Woody would occasionally toss off, but coming from him it sounded worldly, not crass. I was therefore surprised when he told me he'd become serious about a girl and she was coming over to a party later one night. He was nervous all afternoon, which was very unlike the Woody I knew, and I was more than a little curious to meet the girl who had finally snagged him.

Arriving late, she was even more attractive than I imagined. She was petite, with short blonde hair and the body of a ballet dancer, which turned out to be what she was. Although she came as Woody's date, she maintained an air of independence. She was gracious toward Bruce and me all evening, asking us questions in her Georgia sugar-coated voice to make sure we didn't feel left out. It was a typical casual weekend party in Dunster, with weed, wine and music — along with a variety of characters we were starting to know, meandering in and out throughout the evening.

I noticed there was some tension between Woody and his girl as the evening went on. They had a private chat as the party was winding down and when Woody walked away from her, I could see that the conversation did not end well. Noticing me looking at her, she came over to tell me she was leaving. She had been sweet to me all night and something came over me. I asked her if I could go with her and to my amazement she said yes. She took my hand and out the door we went.

We sat on her bed and talked for a while. I knew I was betraying Woody, but the chance that this girl might invite me to bed began to erode any sense of male loyalty. She was getting better looking by the minute and I kept waiting for her to give me a signal. When that didn't come, I finally found the nerve to ask if she wanted to spend the night with me. She gave me a very lovely smile and a genuine look of affection. And then told me no. She apologized if she'd led me on.

So much for my game. I went back to Woody's flat. He was still up and looked hurt. I told him nothing had happened. I thought all would be forgiven. If I had been Woody, I would have given me a little lecture and then another chance. I told him she was still his girlfriend and a virtuous one at that. But it was not to be. In my desire to get laid for the first time, I'd betrayed a mentor and friend. With his usual *savoir faire*, Woody said all the right things, which gave me hope we were still good, but in the end his trust in me was over. After that weekend, I never saw him again.

I was named co-captain of Mr. Briney's JV basketball team at the start of the season. It had less to do with refined basketball skills and more to do with my swagger from playing in so many pickup

I am in the back row, third from the right. I shoved my knee into the back of Allen Black as this photo was taken, which is why we're both smiling.

games. Mr. Briney was short and intense. He wore grey sweat-pants and a whistle around his neck. I liked him at first. Unlike Mr. Gould, my lower mid year basketball coach, he could actually play basketball and would scrimmage with us. But before too long, when we started to play interleague games against other schools, he over-coached as opposed to letting us develop our own chemistry the way Mr. Cobb did. His over-analyzing got to the point where I'd go up for a shot and worry more about what he was thinking than sinking it. I slowly lost my confidence, co-captain status and eventually my starting position.

Gary, Kristin's brother, was also on the team and went in the other direction, working his way up from a sub to a starting position. I liked Gary. Everyone at Taft liked Gary. He fit in so quickly and had so many lower mid friends that we hardly saw each other except for basketball. He was gregarious, athletic and without a mean or petty bone in his body. He looked a little stiff with his back ramrod straight when he went up for a jump shot, but the boy could shoot. And basketball wasn't even his favorite sport — football was. He had an easy-going relaxed charm and

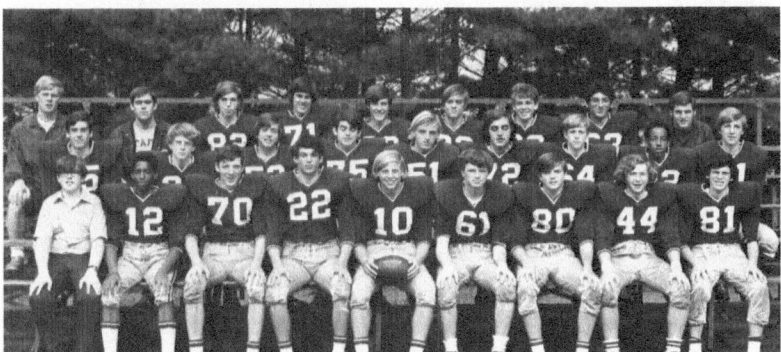

Gary Olson (wearing number 10 in the middle of the front row) turned out to be a stand-out football and basketball player at Taft.

I was surprised and a bit jealous at how easily Gary was navigating his athletic career at Taft. When he asked me which team he should go out for in the fall, I told him to try out for lower school football but not to get his hopes up as a starter. He made the JV football team and then the JV basketball team, both as a starter and then as a rising star — all without trying too hard or taking any of it too seriously. With his long blonde hair, Nordic features and most of all, his large blue eyes, he often reminded me of his sister Kristin. I still thought about her, and sometimes seeing him was a painful reminder of what I'd lost.

One evening after dinner in the middle of the winter term, Gary came up and told me Kristin was on the phone and wanted to speak with me. My heart began to pound, and even though my head told me not to, I went down to the phone booths in the basement. Hearing her voice on the other end of the line brought back all the feelings I had for her, but it quickly became apparent, to me anyway, that she was over me. She was between semesters in college and traveling around the country with a musician. She sounded blissfully happy. A little too blissful, I thought, but I was in no position to question anyone's bliss, least of all hers. I wanted to tell her all the things I'd rehearsed in my head since I last saw her. If not that, at least let her know my own brief encounter with bliss had crawled out her bedroom window the year before. Only that was my problem now, not hers. I couldn't think of anything to say. She told me I would always have a special place in her heart. After my betrayal, the only place I deserved to be in her heart was the dungeon chamber, as far as I was concerned. I wished her well and handed the phone back to Gary.

Mr. Rozelle assigned us *One Flew Over the Cuckoo's Nest* winter term; quashing my "we're not learning anything relevant" argument. The book did, however, confirm that I was on the right path. It was an easy leap to substitute Taft for the mental hospital in Kesey's book. It also confirmed something I already knew. Direct confrontations against Taft got you nowhere except a one-way ticket home. The year before, Grant Goodeve and Robbie Davie (the older brother of Jon Davie, my best friend from my early Middlebury days) had thrown a Molotov cocktail onto the hockey rink late one night in protest. Over what I don't know because I wasn't there. Unfortunately for them, Mrs. Goodeve had sewn Grant's name on the washcloth they used to ignite it.

A year later, it no longer required such stellar detective work for Taft to get rid of its undesirables. Mr. Esty had come up with a new way of weeding out students who hadn't been caught breaking any of its major rules. The new policy was called "Negative Attitude." Which meant if you were perceived to have one, you and your negative attitude could find a new place to dwell.

Our upper-class committee was still largely comprised of the same members from our lower mid year, led by Peter Miller and John Taft. They (along with the other three class committees) continued to act as the liaisons between the administration and students. And they must have been put in an increasingly awkward position as a growing number of students were turning against Taft for policies like "negative attitude." As the winter of 1970 and 1971 progressed, not even Mr. Esty's "Holiday!" did much to relieve the growing discontent. More often than not, there was still nothing else to do on a cold winter "vacation" day except to grouse in our rooms and catch up on homework.

The first Ali-Frasier heavyweight title bout took place that winter. As with most major news, cultural or sporting events, our only access was to listen to the round-by-round recap on radio. To get around this, you had to befriend a master and be invited to his apartment to watch television. Outside of Mr. Marx, the only other time I received an invitation to a master's apartment was one night during winter term from Mr. Barnard. He invited a couple of other boys as well, so his intent did not worry me so much as it made me question: Why was he inviting me? I had no connection to him other than we would have been neighbors in Greenwich if we hadn't moved back to Los Angeles.

It was evening when I showed up along with the two other students whose names I can't recall. We took our seats while Biff threaded a film reel onto a movie projector, making small talk before he dimmed the lights. It was a stag flick with subtitles. Having never see one before, I was as surprised as I was curious. Fifteen minutes later, I'd seen enough. It went from awkward to uncomfortable to slightly nauseating. I begged off early, not wanting to send the wrong message but also not wanting images of sex like that burned into my brain any more than the image I had of me straddling Mr. Marx.

Around the same time, Mr. Rozelle had begun entertaining a young lady in his apartment down the hall. This did not sit well with me or Bruce. It was one thing to know what we were missing. It was another to rub our noses in it. Late one evening, several of us filled a trash can with water and tipped it up against his door. We knocked and ran back to our rooms. A few days later Mr. Rozelle took me aside and told me that his carpet was ruined and we'd nearly drowned his cat. He said he knew I was the ringleader. He learned it was me through another student on our floor, the son of an administrator at the school. To his credit, Mr. Rozelle did not report me as far as I know because I received no formal punishment.

In the wake of that, I decided to downshift my acts of disobedience to removing chalk, erasers and chairs from classrooms in the middle of the night. Writing Free and Rory Gallagher lyrics on the chalkboard in Mr. Barclay's room, giving him something to ponder over his morning coffee. Some faculty children had built a snowman below our room. For a time, it looked cute and then it began to sag and look old and depressing. Deciding to put it out of its misery, we stuck an M-80 in its nose one night. After removing most of the gunpowder from the fuse, we were able to make it back to our room in time to watch Frosty lose his head while we were keeping ours.

Bruce and I continued to be inspired by music. Our tastes overlapped in some areas. We both liked Traffic and Cream, for instance. As a hunter of obscure records and new artists, I brought Ry Cooder's debut album along with Free and some really obscure bands like Gracious and the first King Crimson into the mix. One of Bruce's guilty pleasures was Grand Funk Railroad. While I considered them too commercial, we both liked "I'm Your Captain" — a melodic roller coaster song with the lines "I'm your captain, I'm your captain, though I'm feeling mighty sick" before fading out with the refrain "I'm getting closer to my home" accompanied by the sound of seagulls as their boat approaches the shore at the end of a long voyage. It captured what we were both thinking: our poisonous journey through Taft was coming to an end, one way or another.

Another song we liked was "Something in the Air" by Thunderclap Newman. They were an odd group. One of their members looked distinctly middle-aged, and their music was tin pan alleyish, orchestral and piano-based with fragile, alto vocals that sounded like the singer was recruited out of an all-boys church choir. Which made the lyrics delivered in that one minor hit of theirs all the more powerful:

> Break out the guns and ammo, because there's something
>   in the air.
> We've got to get together sooner or later, because the revolu
>   tion's here.
> And you know it's right, and you know that it's right.
> We have got to get it together, now.

That song was a call to arms, but for the two of us it was more than that. It was also a lament. We knew our days at Taft were numbered and we were fighting a losing battle.

In spite of Mr. Esty's lectures against illegal drugs and his pleading reminders that Taft students seek out "natural highs," he was waging a losing battle of his own. Angel dust, a potent form of pot laced with an anesthetic, made its way onto campus in late winter or early spring and several varsity football players along with other straight-line Tafties let their hair down one night and partied with it. To the point that at least one of them had a severe psychotic reaction. A young admissions officer and English teacher, new to Taft that year, a "do as we say, not as we do" drinking buddy of Mr. Barnard's and Mr. Briney's, left the school under a cloud of suspicion that he'd been caught selling drugs to students. John Dant kept pestering me to get high with him until finally one night we went out and smoked a joint together

in the bitter cold. It was the only time I did that at Taft and I was
extremely nervous about getting caught and thrown out. John
did not seem to be worried at all. By that point John and I were
traveling down different paths at Taft, so it seemed more like we
were making up for something we should have done back when
we were lower mids. I was too paranoid to feel the buzz and John
was John — mellow, easy going and one step ahead of the game.
Looking back, I can imagine the pressure John must have been
under, and why he felt immune that night. Taft must have been
a long, strange trip for John. Faced with an early choice between
seceding from Taft or succeeding at it, John would ultimately
choose the latter.

As winter ebbed into spring, the overall mood at Taft began to
relax. Bruce and I befriended a couple of local girls and would
meet them on weekends out in a field behind Westover, a nearby
private school for girls. I don't remember their real names or
where they went to school. The one I was with called herself Tiger
Lily. After polishing off a bottle or two of Boone's Farm wine,
we'd spend the rest of the afternoon staring up at the clouds or
making out until it was time to get back to Taft.

There were at least thirteen black students at school that year.
There may have been more, but that's how many faces I count in
my '71 yearbook as members of Taft's Afro-American Congress.
There was no let-up to the number of new groups and societies
one could join since my lower mid year. They were like little gold
stars you could tack on to your college application to substantiate
your worth. In addition to the Afro-American Congress, there
was the Annual, Papyrus, Press, Forum, Photography, Community Chest, Debate, Chess, Masque and Dagger, Band, Sailing,

Computer, Glee, Oriocos (*a cappella* singing group), and last but not least — Cheerleaders.

I liked the racial diversity at Taft. I had more in common with and far more interest in getting to know black students like Chris Wolcott than I did wealthy white East Coast preppies. Not that I had anything against white East Coast preppies. I just didn't have much in common with them. I also found people who'd faced adversity more interesting.

While Taft's policy of admitting black and Hispanic students looked progressive on the outside, the reality was mixed. Some were admitted for their athletic ability (as were fifth-year athletic ringers) while others were admitted on their academic merits — in some cases both. But by and large they were all mostly left to their own devices. Once you were admitted to Taft, it was sink or swim, regardless of external factors like your race, upbringing or back story. My former Tower floormate Willie Barley was gone, as was Chris Wolcott. I had no idea what happened to them. There were two blacks on my JV basketball team. They were great teammates. As was Brian Lacy, the senior tight end who understood my frustration when I was relegated to third string behind him and said some nice things to me when I told him I was quitting.

There was obviously still a lot of racism in America. I was raised by parents who did not spout racist beliefs. My mother was especially sensitive to how black people had been treated in America. She gave me several books to read on the subject including *Durango Street* and *Rivers of Blood, Years of Darkness*. By then I may have already read the *Autobiography of Malcolm X* and was blown away by it. As a result of those books and others, along with my own observations, I was empathetic toward black Americans without personally knowing any except for those I met at Taft.

So, while I was aware of the overall sorry treatment of blacks in America, Martin Luther King Jr.'s message, asking people to judge others by the content of their character and not the color of their skin, made perfect sense to me. An easy code to live by in the twentieth century, and simple to remember — basically respect others and treat people as you would like to be treated. It's all you need to know.

Aside from "Jap quizzes," a term widely used by masters and students alike when referring to a surprise quiz, I did not hear any racially charged words at Taft. I don't think there was a single student at Taft who wasn't aware of America's history of slavery and racism. Most of us knew that a disproportionate number of soldiers fighting in Vietnam came from poor or minority families. The war was televised; it was hard to miss. It was also well understood that those with money or the right connections could use college deferments or pay doctors for 4-F classifications to evade the draft. Obviously, the latter would have been an especially delicate subject at a school like Taft. But every student at Taft knew what the score was, and that there was nothing much we could do about it.

Most of us liked and listened to black music, or at the very least were aware of the huge influence black music had on rock and roll. Many of our sports heroes were black. But as with so many other social issues boiling in the late sixties and early seventies, black students felt they needed their own groups to express their solidarity and advocate their own agenda. This happened at Taft in the spring. And as with any action, there was an equal and opposite reaction.

The Afro-American Congress at Taft convened a meeting in a classroom one weekend morning. It happened to be in one of the first-floor classrooms directly below the CPT wing. Just below my room and a few yards from where John Hagelin would have splattered if he'd lost his grip on the gutter above our room. Word of their meeting spread throughout CPT and the reaction was a flash mob. In short order, water balloons were being filled and distributed to every willing and able white student, including me. We opened our windows and yelled down. One of the black students opened the window and looked up as dozens of water balloons rained down. Several of them came running up the stairs a short time later, only to find us sitting at our desks with books open, professing innocence, moral outrage and our offer to help search for the guilty parties.

I'm sure black students at Taft saw this as white bigotry and racism, and perhaps among a small minority, it was just that. But for me, it was an act of rebellion against the school, not them, and a release of the pent-up anger we felt at being exploited ourselves. I'm not sure what the aim of Taft's Afro-American Congress was, but it excluded people like me because of my skin color. Had they been any other minority group looking to better their position at Taft, the reaction would have been the same. For a growing number of us, Taft was the problem, and the solution wasn't to divide ourselves into separate groups and change it from within, but to unite and destroy it from without.

That incident was never brought up in vespers or in the classroom. Either Mr. Esty never became aware of it, which is hard to believe, or he chose to ignore it. By late spring, Taft's mission to achieve excellence in college admissions was the focus again. Like the swallows returning to Capistrano, letters of acceptance were showing up in PO boxes, and seniors were flocking around them.

After spring break, the perks of being seniors played out all over again too. With college admissions in hand, their classes were essentially over. They molted into summertime activities while the rest of us were still bucking up for final exams. As the lawns returned to a welcoming shade of green, seniors would spend weekend afternoons with their girlfriends, enjoying the sunshine or watching a game of lacrosse or baseball, lounging like lions after devouring a fresh kill.

For lower mids and mids like Gary Olson, this ritual must have looked as seductive as it did my lower mid year. Three and a half years of hard work and then you got to take your final semester off. For us upper mids, still grinding away, watching the senior class parade around in holiday dress did not improve our spirits.

Mr. Rozelle's class had its up and downs but aside from Mr. Reiff's biology course lower mid year, his class was the most interesting to me. We had to memorize the opening paragraph of Shakespeare's *Macbeth*, which was tedious, and I could have done without dissecting "Ode on a Grecian Urn." But he did assign us *Armies of the Night* by Mailer and *One Flew Over the Cuckoo's Nest*, which more than made up for what I assume were the mandatory books that UM English had to cover. In one of the last essays Mr. Rozelle assigned, I decided to try a little experiment. I did not study the subject we were supposed to critique and instead made everything up; footnoting references like Janov's *Primal Scream* among other trinkets of manure I'd heard or read about in *Time* or *Newsweek* to bolster my paper. I received a grade of high honors. Proof that the more erudite you sounded at Taft, the sweeter the reward.

CHAPTER 21

Our final mixer at Taft was held on a late spring evening. There were no classes the following day, so it might have been on the eve of one of Mr. Esty's announced holidays or more likely it was on a Saturday night. The mixers were no longer the cattle-call, white-gloved affairs we'd been subjected to my lower mid year. I don't remember the dance but afterward the girls stuck around like they had nowhere to go and were looking for something else to do. It was a pleasant evening and a conga line began streaming up to the Wade where the good times could continue to roll without adult interference. Tiger Lily and her girlfriend intercepted Bruce along the way. They had a bottle or two of Boone's Farm wine. We proceeded to get toasted as we reminisced about our Moody Blues "Tuesday Afternoons" in the fields behind Westover. Up at the Wade there were throngs of boys and girls — laughing, talking, smoking — having a good time celebrating nothing in particular except a rare free moment of our own making with the opposite sex.

A low fog had crept in, leaving the evening humid and warm. Then Mr. Greene arrived, announcing the party was over and we were all to return to Taft's main fortress and get back to our separate camps. Mr. Greene must have drawn the short stick for the assignment, but he assured us reinforcements were on the way. On cue, a light rain began to fall, which put a damper on the evening. We reluctantly quit the Wade and then had to walk past a triumphant Mr. Greene, grinning like Elmer Fudd after ridding rascally rabbits from his carrot patch.

I was walking back down the path toward school with Tiger Lily when there was a clap of thunder and then it started to pour. We took shelter under a bush outside Congdon House. We held each other tight for warmth and after she more or less agreed, I unbuttoned her pants. As things progressed and luck would have it, we didn't break on through to the other side. We abandoned our muck nest and walked back to Taft — two besotted, wet virgins no longer in need of shelter on that wild night.

I don't think I ever saw Tiger Lily again, or even knew her real name. I haven't thought about her much over the years except for this. Even though what happened that night seemed consensual to me, it might not have seemed so consensual to her. I do remember how my thoughts unfolded, starting with run-of-the-mill lust, before flashing onto the thought this might be my opportunity to prove once and for all that Mr. Marx's rumor about me couldn't be true. That was the main goal of mine for coming back and I briefly saw Tiger Lilly as my ticket to redemption that night while we were fumbling in the mud. As we were walking back hand in hand, I realized how stupid that thought was. And that redemption no longer mattered to me.

As punishment for our misbehavior at the Wade House, our hours there were cut back. Several of us liked watching television and relaxing there, so when the new restricted hours were announced, it upset a lot of upper mids. Spending weekend afternoons drinking and necking with our girlfriends that spring had mellowed Bruce and me. We'd even signed up for a Taft volunteer activity, a neighborhood drive where we towed a red wagon around Watertown collecting old newspapers for God knows what reason other than it was always good to get off the grounds. When our class committee proved ineffective at reversing the new Wade House hours, student opposition got heated, and Bruce and I found ourselves back in our regular line of business at Taft: orchestrating trouble.

Our reputation as instigators was well known, and our room became the place for outraged students to gather, vent and plot. A decision was made. We would hold a protest at the Wade. We radiated out from room to room, evading the known snitches as we made our pitch against tyranny and picked up converts, until we had more than enough — and then volunteers began asking if they could join. We agreed to stage the sit-in at the Wade the following Saturday night. By Saturday day we were worn out from the planning and half defeated with worry.

Our walk up to the Wade House that evening was all about nerves. Many students who vowed to be there had lost theirs and understandably so. The twenty to twenty-five students who did make the long walk knew they were potentially risking their careers at Taft.

The Wade House was a large, simple one-room log cabin, with a stone fireplace, an elevated black and white TV and three or four wooden picnic tables. It was normally a relaxing place — with old furniture and knick-knacks left behind by departed seniors — but not that night. I'm not even sure we had time to smoke a cigarette to calm our nerves before the clock struck 10 and we were officially breaking curfew. Our conversations became whispers and then the whispers petered out as we all stared at the door and waited.

The heavy footfall we were expecting came soon enough. In walked Dean Oscarson. He had the annoyed look of a bear whose hibernation had been interrupted. Looking at the faces in front of him, he started writing down the names of certain boys before tucking his notepad back in his breast pocket. Having sorted the perpetrators from the followers, he matter-of-factly told us all to get out. No one moved. This surprised him.

Bruce and I were sitting at the table farthest from him. Mr. Oscarson ran his fat fingers through his slicked black hair and, as if to give us the benefit of the doubt that we hadn't heard him the first time, repeated "GET OUT." His delivery a little less charitable than before. There were a few flinches but no one got up. What he thought was a weak showing by a bunch of coddled students was turning out to be more than he expected.

Facing solidarity, Mr. Oscarson heaved the heavy sigh of the king's appointed guardian of the realm. Did we not understand he was just sitting down to a horsemeat pie back in his merry Taft apartment, when news of a peasant revolt was whispered in his ear? Apparently not.

He looked around and chose his first "volunteer." Anthony Pasqualini, an unassuming kid who preferred acting to sports, happened to be sitting closest to him. Anthony was hauled to his feet before what a laconic reporter might call "his forced removal from the premises." The air was charged after that. All eyes were on Oscie, red-faced and sweating now. Our beloved dean — dropping his honeysuckle composure and reverting to some pre-Taft atavistic instinct that lay below the surface. He looked almost as shocked by what he'd done to Anthony as we were. The clock continued to tick and still no one moved. We had the moral upper hand on him now and he seemed to sense it. But he was in so deep he was out of options. With no way out except to plow ahead and remove us one by one. Only after he began to scan the room for his next victim did we start to break ranks. If we were going to watch a rerun of what he did to Pasqualini, there was no reason to stay.

As news of what happened spread the next day, a sort of pall hung over the school. That night marked the beginning of the end of open resistance to Taft's authority. For everyone there that night, there were only a handful who were willing to continue risking their careers when the sun came up the next day. When punishments were handed down, Bruce, I and a few others received a stayover. Parents of students who got off with a warning were probably feeling more generous than usual when the next annual fundraiser request came in the mail.

There were only a few weeks left of school and the muggy stultifying days of Connecticut were upon us. It was hard enough to study when so much of it seemed irrelevant, and harder still when the outdoors beckoned or it was just too hot and humid to want to do anything except rest, read a book or listen to music. There was some talk about hiding the chairs lined up on the lawn the night before senior graduation, but after our stand at the Wade, that seemed a little anticlimactic.

On the following Saturday afternoon before graduation, an impromptu stickball game broke out on the lawn below our room. Small at first, it quickly drew a crowd. Each batter became more outrageous in his swing, trash talk and attire — or lack of it, at risk of being booed out of the batter's box if he didn't ham it up enough. It became theater, and began drawing the interest of students who wandered over from Mr. Stone's varsity baseball game to see what was going on. No one kept score and anyone who wanted could play. The game went on until dusk, drawing in over half the school by the time it was over. Russian baseball had come to Taft.

Late one Sunday afternoon I got word that I was wanted up in Mike Castillo's room. I'd never really cottoned to Mike, still sore after he publicly called me out for pretending to be a surfer my lower mid year. He was a star soccer player, and arguably the best-looking boy in our class. I presumed he was looking forward to his senior year when, for the first time in its existence, Taft would become a coed school.

There were several upper mids in his room when I arrived, among them Whit Gray, Bruce's old roommate, with his shirt open and a crude drawing of a knife or cross penned on his bare chest in homage to Black Sabbath. Chris Minor, a varsity football player disillusioned with Taft, was also there. Above the door as I came in was Peter Sutphen, a human spider who climbed walls and could remain suspended and walk his way across the ceiling of a hallway unnoticed. Some gifts at Taft were appreciated more than others.

Mike's room was at the end of a hall that faced west and looked down on the main driveway in the front of the school. A dozen eggs sat on the coffee table. Someone motioned me over to the window and pointed to a red car parked in the driveway below.

Whit Gray, fellow upper mid, 1971

It belonged to Mr. Rozelle and why I'd been invited became clear. They all thought I should do the honors and be the first to egg his car. They knew I'd ragged on him all year. They were more than a little surprised when I declined. In my mind, I'd put Mr. Rozelle through enough already. As I started to walk away, Whit said to me "Come on, Coe. Ten years from now you'll look back and laugh. You know, like you always say." That had been my mantra at Taft all year and I would often use it to get others to join me in some prank. But for some reason my own line didn't work on me. I'd done a lot of things to undermine Taft and earn the reputation I wanted. I felt I'd succeeded, if you could call it that, and it was time to move on. I went back to my room.

Nothing came of it until the last day of school, when Mr. Rozelle took me aside in the hallway. He told me his car had been shelled and he suspected me. Based on past performance, I could understand why. When I denied it and turned to go, he pressed on, threatening to get me thrown out of Taft if I didn't own up to it. Once again, I told him I had nothing to do with it. His threats were starting to erode any sympathy over the way I'd treated him. He was still part of Taft's power structure, demanding answers for something I hadn't done. As far as I was concerned, he could find his answers elsewhere. He would not let it go. Telling me that if I hadn't done it, I knew who did. I liked him as a teacher; respected him for not giving up on me and for his encouragement in class despite my antics. If I'd been him, I would have given up and tossed me out of his class a long time ago.

I would have liked for him to know what it was like living across the hall from Mr. Marx when I was 14. How the experience shaped me into who I was. That the person before him didn't give a rat's ass about getting thrown out and in fact looked forward to it. Getting expelled would be the crowning achievement of my Taft career. He was doing me the ultimate favor without knowing it. These thoughts went through my mind as he tried to leverage his power as a master to break me. It was getting boring. Our time was up. He gave me one last chance to become a rat and I refused.

This exchange took place as the exodus of students was underway and most seniors were out on the town celebrating with parents and friends, waiting for next day's graduation ceremony. I went back up to my room. Bruce put on Alice Cooper and we opened the window and blasted out their testosterone-soaked anthem "I'm Eighteen." I don't know about Bruce but I was still 16 at the time. I think we both felt a bit older and wiser than our years.

Our stayover job was to remove chewing gum from underneath the dining room tables. When we turned the first table over on

John C. Esty, Jr., headmaster of the Taft School, during my time there..

its side, the number of dried wads made clear gum chewing was as epidemic at Taft as drugs. We were handed kitchen knives, but they proved no match for the epoxy-like bonding we were up against. After complaining that the job would take all summer, our tools were upgraded to small hammers and chisels.

It was extremely warm and in no time at all we were, as Chick Hearn, the Lakers' radio announcer often said, "perspiring freely."

The staff, 'Bo's' and 'Bats' as they were commonly referred to at Taft, came in and out the kitchen doors with platters of food in preparation for the upcoming post-graduation party, eyeing us with a mixture of pity and distrust. All year long you could read the resentment in their tight smiles as you picked up your laundry while the boilers rumbled and the presses hissed behind them, or when they doled out our food from the steam tables in their sweat-stained white uniforms and hairnets. It wasn't until you were punished and forced to join their ranks by peeling potatoes or scraping gum that their expressions softened a bit. You were given a glimpse of what their lives were like. One of them left a pitcher of ice water out for us on the sly.

Mr. Oscarson came around every now and again to check on our work. He was back to being his benevolent light-hearted self and made little quips while cheerily reminding us that however many days it took, we couldn't leave school until the job was done. He would pirouette with a flourish, and the hollow tapping of our knives and chisels would resume.

The dining room floor was the same red terra cotta tile as the main hallway. It reflected noise rather than absorbed it. There were four or five of us chipping away, and every now and again, our banging would synchronize, sounding strangely crude and a little like a Stone Age rhythm section. After several such interludes, a weird thing happened. For some reason, the Grateful Dead song "Easy Wind" popped into our heads, perhaps because of its strong percussive beat or the long road ahead with the work we were doing. We all tapped into it. Our tools became drumsticks and tables became our drums. We sang that song in one endless loop for hours. At the end of the second day Mr. Oscarson told us we were done and could leave the next morning. We protested that we hadn't finished the job and volunteered to stay on but he was having none of it. He was sick of our music, sick of our attitude and probably more than anything, sick of our smiling, dirty, defiant faces.

On my last day at Taft, Mr. Barnard came up to me with a grim look as I waited for my grandparents to pick me up and take me to the airport to fly back to Los Angeles. Aside from his invitation to watch the stag film at his apartment earlier that year, I never got to know him and never really cared to. He seemed more interested in legacy students and remaining connected to them after Taft. Despite his Machiavellian tendencies, he was otherwise an okay guy. Compared to Mr. Marx he was a saint, but by the same token he, like all the other masters at Taft, was either blind or looked the other way when it came to Mr. Marx, Mr. Jacobs and who knows how many others masters who were like them. For that reason, I did not trust him, so I was a little surprised when he took me aside.

In the brief conversation that followed, he told me the student review meeting had just wrapped up. He explained how the

masters gathered at the end of each school year and went down
a list of all the students. If one of them raised an objection about
a student, they would all take a vote. He said he was sorry, but
that I would not be invited back senior year. I thanked him for
the heads up.

Word came that my grandparents were parked outside. I walked
down the main corridor, past the honor roll board, the adminis-
trative offices and Mr. Esty's office for the last time. Pausing at
the steps that led down to the dining hall anteroom, I glanced
up at the HDT staircase that Bruce and I had tiptoed down so
many nights on our way to ISP. Underneath one of the steps,
some lower mid had scrawled my last name in chalk. It made
me feel good knowing what we did wasn't all in vain. That some
lower classman understood what we were trying to do and would
hopefully carry on the resistance. And that Mr. Esty would likely
see it when he stepped out of his office.

Not long after returning to California, I casually mentioned to
my parents that I was not going to be asked back. My mother
did not believe me. I was used to that by then, but I still had to
go through the formal process of explaining why.

Had I flunked out? Had I been caught cheating or using drugs or
alcohol? When I answered no, she found it impossible to believe.
They hadn't received any letters of warning. I shrugged as if to say
Taft works in mysterious ways and to be prepared just in case.
When the formal letter of dismissal came at the end of June, she
flew into a mild rage when my father got home from work. She
demanded my father fly her back to receive an explanation from

Mr. Esty in person. I'd fulfilled my mission at Taft. For me it was over. For my mother the gloves were off and back they went.

When my parents returned, they were rather meek in reporting what happened. Giving them fifteen minutes of his time, Mr. Esty told them I had "hung out with the wrong crowd." When my mother asked him who let the "wrong crowd" into Taft in the first place, he apparently had trouble finding an answer. That gave my parents leverage and Mr. Esty agreed to change my record from "dismissed" to "voluntarily withdrew." Having that change on my record would make a world of difference when applying for college. That satisfied my parents. If that was all they wanted, and sadly I knew it was when they told me this, I could have saved them the trip. Once I passed the age of truancy, there was no way I would ever let another teacher pass judgment on me again.

PART 8

Living in the Past

Ten years later, in May of 1982, I was heading back to the northeast on a business trip. One of the unforeseen consequences of the change to my record was I became a bona fide Taft alumnus. This led to several perks that I don't think were meant for me. I received the *Taft Alumni Bulletin* four times a year, along with other news, donation requests and invitations to swell cocktail parties hosted by Taft alumni who'd ended up in La-La land. An invitation to attend our ten-year class reunion coincided with my business trip. I couldn't resist. It would be the first time I had anything to do with Taft since I left.

The party for the Class of '72 was held at Molly Baldridge's house. She'd entered the Taft class of '72 as a senior. My parents knew her parents from Middlebury, and I'd probably last seen Molly at summer camp at the Highfield Country Club, where my friends and I would chase and terrorize girls with sharpened popsicle sticks. John Dant was supposed to be there but called at the last minute to say he couldn't make it. John was missed in more ways than one. The party could have used more people. Several faces were new to me, and the ones I did recognize were not part of the resistance that had taken place when I was there. People were friendly, the food was good, there was plenty to drink. There was laughter and reminiscing. But there was something missing. It lacked soul.

It felt surreal going back to Taft the next day. Amid all the class parades, I tried my best to be friendly, but what I missed most kept coming back to me. Where were all my old pals like Bruce? Was I the only one who'd decided to forgive and forget what Taft had been like so we could get together one more time? As the gladhanding and backslapping wore on, I felt like a party crasher at a country club I didn't belong to.

Mr. Lance Odden had taken over as headmaster from Mr. Esty. He was as short, balding and energetic as I remembered — meeting and greeting alumni with the same fervor he had when he was Taft's hockey coach. After the socializing and schmoozing, we were invited to a gathering indoors where Mr. Odden would give a big speech. The line to get in was long but I eventually reached the top step, where Mr. Odden was beaming, shaking everyone's hand, and saying a few words to each person in line like a seasoned politician. When I was finally up, I watched his expression change as he worked out who I was. He ignored my outstretched hand, said nothing, and then smoothly turned to greet the next person in line. I realized I'd just been snubbed. During my two years at Taft, I'd never had any interactions with him, good or bad. As I took a seat to listen to his speech, another thought landed. While I'd forgiven Taft, Taft had apparently not forgiven or forgotten me.

Lance Odden, who was Assistant Headmaster during my years at Taft and would succeed Mr. Esty as Taft Headmaster in 1973

The chapter on all this might have closed once and for all if Mr. Odden had only followed through on his snub and had my name scrubbed off the alumni list. He didn't. And so, I continued to receive the alumni bulletins, invitations to cocktail parties, ballots for new trustees, and most amusing to me, mail imploring me to help Taft meet its annual fund and financial goals. Mr. Barnard was the only former Taft administrator or master who reached out to me in the ensuing years. He was living in San Francisco, contacting former students to drum up investment opportunities in his firm.

The *Taft Bulletin* became glossier over time. It would open with comments from Mr. Odden — often repeating a speech he had given at vespers. It would then spotlight the accomplishments of alumni. That would be followed by news of each class compiled by the class secretary, memorials about the recently departed, milestones of marriages and births and a fiscal report on the Taft Fund: how much money each class had raised and how much more was needed to expand the campus and make capital improvements to ensure it remained in the front ranks of private schools. Lastly, a return envelope to make those dreams come true.

The class of '69, Woody Chase's class, was the most active in terms of reporting in. News from the classes of 1970 and 1971 was meager. Contributions from the class of 1972 were practically nil. There were times when only one or two classmates contributed and several times there was nothing but our class secretary's byline. The class of '72 was the low point. After that class, participation picked up again. I often wondered if other alumni noticed this. Even to a casual observer, unlike me, it would be hard to miss.

Life dealt cruel blows to the former 1971 and 1972 Taft head monitors. Both would be involved in fatal car accidents in the mid-eighties. John Pollak, in the class ahead of mine, would lose an eye, and his best friend at Taft, Rob Holliday, would lose his life while trying to pass a cement truck on a highway. My dear old friend John Dant would be killed in a similar accident in Wyoming a short time later.

Shortly before his accident, which his wife and young daughter survived, I saw John for the last time in San Francisco. We had not been in touch for many years. My girlfriend and I were headed up there and I contacted him. He suggested we meet for breakfast. He walked into the café with the aid of a cane. John was an investment banker with Merrill Lynch. His hair had gone completely gray; his movements were measured and slow. He seemed glad to see me but at arm's length. He spoke slowly, with long, guarded pauses. His wife was with him. She was polite but did not seem interested in a trip down memory lane. I could tell she was proud of John and cherished him, but she seemed to be there almost to protect him. From me or from the past or maybe both. When we left, I told my girlfriend how shocked I was at how old he looked.

Gone was the free-spirited John I'd known at Taft and from the car camping trip we took up through Oregon and Northern California in the summer of 1971. We camped along the Rogue, Deschutes and Mackenzie rivers, played harp and guitar, and spent time at several hippie communes along the way. John did not have much to say about Taft. I'd heard that as head monitor, he had to pass judgment on students who broke the rules, as he once had. Soon after he died, I read that a bronze bust of him was unveiled at Taft in his honor. It seemed like such a hollow gesture to me. Like the theater award named for Bill Waldron. Taft using its fallen to burnish its legacy.

In 1990 I came across another piece of news in the *Bulletin*. Under "Milestones" was a short obituary of Russell Pais, the senior who'd helped me back to my room following my ISP drinking binge lower mid year. It did not list the cause of death but what it did report gave me a small chill. He died in San Francisco, where the AIDS epidemic was just then exploding.

I received the fall 1991 *Alumni Bulletin* with my usual upbeat curiosity as to how few members of the Class of '72 would report in. But this issue had something that captured all my attention: an interview with John Esty. In it, he remembered his tenure at Taft during the late '60s as a "terrible time," and pointedly mentioned rich, spoiled students who "regularly kicked poorly paid" teachers around.

I felt fortunate to have missed a school like that. So, I wrote him a long letter describing my school which happened to be his school. It took me several months to write. I had to keep stopping because I'd shake with anger when describing Mr. Marx. He wrote back that he did seem to recall me, and that my time there did not seem to be "a happy one for me." As for my descriptions of Mr. Marx, he was left with the question of why I didn't tell anyone in the adult community at the time. He added he would keep our correspondence and consider it an important archival note on his years at Taft.

I showed my letter to him to my parents. I thought it might fill in some blanks about me for them. They stopped reading after the second paragraph. They didn't want to hear it. I got the impression they thought my story was an indictment of them. That I was using it as an excuse for turning out the way I did. All things considered, I thought I turned out okay, and, by then, hurting them was the last thing I wanted to do. I saw their point, however. They didn't want to be blamed for something that happened a long time ago, when they were only trying to provide a better opportunity for me. They also had enough on their plate between running a small business and keeping up with the demands of everyday life. Several weeks later, as an olive branch, my mother confided that they had been introduced to someone at a dinner party, years earlier, an exchange teacher from England who'd taught at Taft for a year after I'd left. He told her he quit, with little to say other than Taft was "a nightmare."

I forwarded the two letters I wrote Mr. Esty to *60 Minutes* and the *Boston Globe*, hoping someone would read them and find them worth an investigation. Neither responded.

In 2016, I received a letter sent to Taft alumni, admitting the school had hired (and subsequently fired) a master who had been caught molesting students at another prep school. I exchanged a couple of emails with Taft's then headmaster, Mr. MacMullen, now recently retired, describing my school experience. Mr. McMullen apologized on behalf of the school, and then assured me that Taft was currently a very fine place. Adding as an aside that as an alumnus, I missed a golden opportunity to send my son or daughter there. I wanted to tell him getting into Taft was easy. It was getting out that was hard.

I've thought a lot about Mr. Marx over the years. Adults like him are often interesting — especially to young, curious minds, like mine was back then. He was cunning, and Taft provided him the perfect cover to hide demons that were, at times, beyond his control. He was smart enough to know that Taft would have to defend him against any accusations. Any accusation against him would be an accusation against the school. And if that had happened, if I had come forward back in an era when that was unheard of — Taft had far more to lose than he did. The following is from the Taft 1966 yearbook:

> Walter Herman Marx, AMT Latin. Mr. Marx, a new member of Taft's Classics Department, is from Jamaica Plain, Massachusetts. He prepared for college at the Roxbury Latin School, graduating in 1957. He then entered Harvard, where he majored in Latin and minored in Greek. He received his undergraduate degree in 1961 and continued his studies at Harvard, earning his Master of Arts in Teaching In 1962. In 1963 and 1964 he taught at the St. Stephens Episcopal School in Austin, Texas. In the Summer of 1965, he received a Fulbright Grant to study at the American Academy in Rome and then traveled to Naples for additional study. In the fall of 1966, following his sojourn In Europe, Mr. Marx came to Taft.

The following illustrates how real his demons were, and why I never saw him again after our encounter in the school hallway in the fall of 1970:

Email from Dick Cobb (my former soccer coach) to Robert Foreman (Taft alumnus and one of my editors) from 2012:

> Walter Marx is indeed a sad story. In the winter of the 1970-71 school year, he was talked down from a skyscraper they were building in NYC. He went back to Massachusetts to his parents' place, eventually got a job at one of the Boston area private schools (and published some stuff — which is how I know this part of the story), but then was found dead in the attic of his parents' house (as I found out from Dan Comiskey after Dan retired and moved to MA). Not a hundred percent sure, but it sounds to me like Walter succeeded in this attempt. That's all the news that's fit to print, and some that isn't.

Mr. William Jacobs, the master who returned my broom in the middle of the night my lower mid year, taught chemistry and physics at Taft from 1965 to 1971. In 2012, the *Minneapolis Star Tribune* printed the following story:

> Newly released investigative records reveal years of missed opportunities to stop a serial child molester. In probing what would become one of the most disturbing cases of serial child molestation in Minnesota, the detectives also uncovered a history of missed opportunities and reluctance to expose a potential scandal.

According to the investigative file, obtained by the
Star Tribune under the Minnesota Data Practices Act,
the detectives learned that in the early 1970s, Jacobs
had lost as many as three teaching jobs because he
fondled children, yet in each case, his supervisors kept
the situations quiet. In a deposition he gave last May
in exchange for being dropped from a victim's lawsuit,
Jacobs said he was confronted by the headmaster for
inappropriately "approaching" at least one student.
Jacobs quietly left the school in 1971. Taft spokes-
woman Julie Reiff said the school "has no knowledge
of any improper conduct by Mr. Jacobs while at Taft."
(courtesy Abby Simons)

As I said at the beginning, my reason for writing this memoir
was to respond to Mr. Esty's 1991 interview in the *Taft Bulletin*.
These are the excerpts from his interview that stood out to me:

I think teachers are the *sine qua non* of good education,
of good schools. The big challenge is for teachers to
go on devotedly teaching when it's so damn hard, the
hours are so long, and a lot of teachers get kicked
around.... I'll never forget the time at Taft a mother
approached me to complain that her son's teachers
seemed hard on him, while "all the other servants think
he's wonderful..." My experience at Taft was an incredibly rewarding, satisfying, rich, wonderful experience,
and it was really tough at times because it spanned
the troublesome years of 1963 to 1972. For some —
especially teachers and parents — that was a time of
unmitigated horror. In actual fact, I thought it was

pretty horrible. To me one of the most disappointing things was that a basic tenet of my philosophy, trust — one which I practiced as a parent, and tried to carry with me to Taft — eroded very quickly in the midst of the rising drug culture. Trust is given and then earned, but it gets given first, and if there is a sense that it won't be earned, or that kids can't be trusted, that's incredibly erosive.... there's a very important distinction to be made between the exogenous pressures — the external events in society — and what one school was doing to fend off the preposterous, hurtful things. I will be sorry if historians of that period think that the turbulence ruined Taft when part of the internal turbulence was ordinary growing pains — the evolving, growing, developing of a school.... I knew that it is the head of the school who's really critical. I never lost my partisanship for the school head in NAIS, and I think they understood that and appreciated that. That came right from my Taft headmastership.

NAIS stands for National Association of Independent Schools. Mr. Esty was head of that organization for thirteen years. He authored several books, including *Choosing a Private School*. He passed away in 2016. After our letter exchanges in 1992, I never heard from him again. As for Mr. Esty "keeping our correspondence and considering it an important archival note on his years at Taft," I don't know where they ended up. Although I have a pretty good guess.

PART 9

Aftermath

CHAPTER 23

I graduated Palisades High School in June 1972. I worked at a ranch in Wyoming right after that. I had no desire to continue my formal education. The art of disruption I'd practiced at Taft went away as soon as I left. I never took part in any protest marches or subversive activities after Taft. I watched some of the Watergate hearings on television but corruption didn't interest me. Getting away from it did.

I roamed around the country for a while. I was a dropout. Trying to find a place far from a city where I could do something simple, like farm. But that proved difficult. The optimism of the counter-culture was receding. Hippie communes, one of the earliest and more promising examples of sixties idealism, were regressing into squabbling fiefdoms thanks in part to cult leaders like Charles Manson. Affordable land took money and I didn't have any. Broke but not broken, I started working for my father in 1975. All I ever wanted to do was work hard at something, and that something turned out to be making boilers. Life has a funny way of working out. I've found that by keeping an open mind, there is always a path forward, as long as you stay true to yourself, and don't forget your hopes and dreams.

This story would not exist without Bruce Maclean and Kristin Olson. Bruce was there in the trenches with me at Taft. And when trenches got overrun by the insanity, he jumped right into the foxhole with me. He was kicked out of Taft after his upper mid year. I don't think he regretted it any more than I did. I couldn't have asked for a better friend. Bruce is a professional guitar player and lives in Cape Cod.

When things were good between us, like they were in Aspen, Kristin would sometimes look at me in a trembly, vulnerable way. Like I had answers she was looking for, and she was half afraid and half ready to tell me what her dreams were. When someone looks at you like that, you have two choices: run or let them in. I had no means to nurture something like that. I wasn't even sure there was a something more than our two little ships passing in the night. So I was stuck between giving her up and not wanting to let her go. And what looked so promising one day became a complicated mess the next. But she left me with an image of what two people who care about each other should look like. I knew if I ever wanted to be looked at that way again, I would have to find my own way. And earn whatever it was to keep it alive. Kristin is a yoga instructor and currently lives in Palm Springs. Along with Bruce, she was kind enough to allow me to write down my memories of her.

A final word about the writing of this book. In 1981 I was living on the island of Ponape, working maintenance at The Village Hotel in Micronesia. That would turn out to be my final attempt at dropping out. If you can call living on one of the most beautiful islands in the world "dropping out." But while there, I began to question why I had this tendency, and realized it was because I had a deep distrust of people and a rather negative attitude about society too. I was curious where that came from and quickly traced it to my experiences at Taft. I wrote to the school and asked if they would send my yearbooks and a copy of the student handbook. I needed to figure out where I was if I was ever going to change. Waiting for the materials to arrive, I began writing down memories, but that's as far as I got. My incompetence as a handyman caught up with me and I was on the road again.

Eleven years later, I was back in Los Angeles. Taft still percolated in the back of my mind, but I was too busy earning a living to give it much thought. This story would have probably remained untold if I hadn't read John Esty's interview. In 1992 I met my future wife, Jennifer, at our twentieth high school reunion. We were married in 1993 and she has been my rock ever since. My life felt complete and on stable ground for the first time in a long time, with one exception – Taft still lurked in the back of my mind. Married, with two young children and running a small business left me with almost no time to write. I dabbled with writing this as a novel based on a favorite short story of mine, "Leiningen Versus the Ants." I wanted to expand on that concept and somehow include Taft. I wanted to explain *why* someone would be motivated to drop out and live on a plantation in the middle of a jungle as a phalanx of army ants prepares to bear down on him. This exercise for a few minutes each night before bedtime kept the story alive in my head. But after twenty to twenty-five years of tinkering with it, I realized I didn't have the chops to write it as a novel.

My father passed away in 2007 and my mother in 2020. We never did talk about Taft after I showed them the letters I wrote to Mr. Esty. For my parents, Taft was like an illness long passed, whose causes and effects were no longer in anyone's best interest to remember. Meanwhile I had grown more objective about it. I thought it was an interesting story on its own merits, with several themes, including family dynamics, that might interest people outside of prep school. After my mother passed away, I thought I'd give it one last try, this time telling it straight and as it happened. Prior to that, I thought the real story was too convoluted to set it all down. But I wasn't getting any younger, and I knew what I wrote could no longer hurt my parents. I think that last part was the key that unblocked me because something clicked. I began writing one weekend late in 2021 and found that telling it straight seemed to work. Writing on the weekends also gave my mind a chance to repair itself during the rest of the week. Obviously, there was a fair amount of pain and some hard truths I had to face when writing about the boy I once was.

ACKNOWLEDGMENTS

All the great music and the musicians from the 1960s. In tribute, I chose Jethro Tull's first album *This Was* for the opening part. Followed by Blodwyn Pig's *Getting to This, Beggars Banquet* for the Rolling Stones, *Looking Through A Glass Onion* for the Beatles, *In Search Of The Lost Chord* for the Moody Blues, *A Shiny Light Breaking Through The Storm* for Joni Mitchell, *Something in the Air* for Thunderclap Newman, *Living in the Past*, for Tull again and finally back to the Stones for *Aftermath*.

Thanks to the following for their comments and support: Bruce Maclean, Kristin Olson, Alex Dominick, Pete Miller, Peter Sutphen, Bob Rozelle, Luci (Waldron) Chorley, Virginia Stancs and Joan B. Atwood.

My wife Jennifer for her love and understanding of what this story has meant to me — and help whenever my computer tried to eat this story.

Royal Calkins for editing. Robert Gutierrez for legal review.

Su-E Tan for cover artwork.

Robert Foreman for his enthusiasm, support, advice, editing, archival contributions and deep knowledge about all things Taft.

ABOUT THE AUTHOR

At Snake River Ranch, Wyoming, July 1972. Photo: Wernher Krutein

www.ingramcontent.com/pod-product-compliance
Lightning Source LLC
Chambersburg PA
CBHW020434130626
46549CB00001B/130